MOTORCYCLES

BP
BP
TOTAL

MOTORCYCLES

CHARLES E. DEANE

Sundial

CONTENTS

First published in Great Britain in 1978 by
Sundial Publications Limited,
59 Grosvenor Street, London W1

Fifth impression, 1980

ISBN 0 904230 59 7

Produced by Mandarin Publishers Limited
22a Westlands Road, Quarry Bay, Hong Kong

Printed in Hong Kong

INTRODUCTION

I've been interested in the history of motorcycles since I was a kid, so I was delighted to be asked to write an introduction to this beautifully produced book. It will fill a long-standing gap on my bookshelf and, I think, on those of many other enthusiasts.

The first bike I ever rode–when I was five years old!–was a Ducati 50 cc, and my first racing machine was a 125 cc Bultaco. Today I ride a Suzuki GS750. All these marques and many others–from earliest times to the present day, from mopeds to superbikes–you will find in these pages.

Over the last few years motorcycling has become much more socially acceptable. It remains, as ever, a cheap and reliable means of getting from here to there. But, every year, thousands more people from every walk of life are discovering that motorbikes offer the most exhilarating form of transport in the world. And motorcycle racing of every kind, from classic GP events to moto-cross, is currently attracting enormous crowds everywhere. This comes as no surprise to me. I think it's the greatest sport of all–and this book shows you the reasons why.

The First Seventy Years

ON 10 November 1885 a rickety looking, timber-framed bicycle, powered by a ½-horsepower, single-cylinder engine, made its maiden run in Bad Cannstatt, near the city of Stuttgart. This curious machine, the brainchild of Gottlieb Daimler, a German gunsmith-turned-engineer, heralded a revolution in transport. But a revolution of what kind? After all, the industrialized world was by this time humming with engines: the railways were more than 60 years old; steamships had progressed to the era of the luxury liner; the first manned and powered airship had already taken to the air. Even on the roads a variety of powered vehicles had made an appearance—steam carriages as long ago as the 1830s.

The revolutionary element in Daimler's machine—as in the almost exactly contemporary Petrolcycle of an Englishman, Edward Butler—was the nature of its engine, which worked on the principle known as internal combustion. Whereas steam engines tend to increase in efficiency with size (hence their success as the power units in ships and trains), Daimler's engine pointed the way towards the evolution of small engines with a high power-to-weight ratio. It was just such engines that made possible the development of *personal* transport vehicles—the motorcycle and the car—that have transformed everyday life in the 20th century.

LEFT Fresh-air transport for the Quality: a Holden autocycle with rickshaw trailer, about 1898. Colonel Holden's design was powered by a water-cooled engine in which the two cylinders had combustion chambers at both ends. Power was delivered directly from the pistons to the rear wheel by crank rods.

Daimler's *Petroleum-Reitwagen* (petrol-driven vehicle) was the progenitor of both the motorcycle and the motorcar. Its engine was based on a type developed in the 1870s by Dr Nikolaus Otto, for whom Daimler had worked for a time. The Otto Cycle, as this engine was called, operated, like the modern car engine, on a four-stroke system, the 'strokes' referring to the movements of a piston within its cylinder: a downward stroke, in which petrol vapour is drawn into the cylinder; an upward stroke in which the vapour is highly compressed; a downward stroke powered by the explosive ignition of the vapour; and an upward stroke in which the spent gases from the explosion are expelled from the cylinder. The vapour enters, and the exhaust leaves, the cylinder by means of valves in the cylinder head.

Although Daimler had clearly shown the way forward in the evolution of the motorcycle, he himself was primarily interested in motorcar manufacture: his colleague and co-builder of the *Reitwagen*, the engineering genius Wilhelm Maybach, was to design the classic Mercedes cars of the first two decades of the 20th century. It was not until 10 years after Daimler's machine had first shown its paces that motorcycle pioneers in France, Germany, and England abandoned their fruitless search for a viable steam-powered bike and turned to internal combustion. Among the leading figures in France to make the switch were Comte Albert de Dion and his partner Georges Bouton, who in 1895 built a tricycle powered by a petrol engine capable of running at an astonishing 1,500 rpm (revolutions per minute)–

BELOW This 1898 Werner $\frac{3}{4}$ hp motorcycle, with engine over the front wheel, was among the earliest French motorcycles to be imported into England.

BOTTOM LEFT The Cudell De Dion of 1898 was based on the tricycles of Comte Albert de Dion and his partner, Georges Bouton, who were among the pioneers of motorized transport in Europe.

BOTTOM RIGHT A 1910 Harley-Davidson single-cylinder, 480 cc Model 6A, one of the type known among workers at Harley's Milwaukee factory as the 'Silent Gray Fellow'. The first of the famous 45-degree V-twin, 1,000 cc models, upon which Harley's later fortunes were founded, was introduced in 1909.

RIGHT The Werner brothers were among the first motorcycle manufacturers to design a machine with the motor positioned low between the wheels. This 1903 Werner motorcycle established design principles that helped greatly to improve stability and controllability at all speeds.

almost double the shaft speed of Daimler's engine. In Germany at about the same time the firm of Hildebrand & Wolfmüller designed a water-cooled two-cylinder petrol-engined bike; while in England Colonel Henry Holden produced a four-cylinder model—or, rather, a two-cylinder model with pistons at both ends of each cylinder.

The firm of De Dion, Bouton et Cie made an important contribution to motorcycling in the closing years of the 19th century. It began to produce 'over-the-counter' engines for a great variety of vehicles, selling them or licensing their production in England, Belgium, Germany, and the United States. (It was one of these engines that in 1898 launched the career of Louis Renault, founder of what was to become the world's first car-manufacturing giant.)

Like all other internal-combustion engines of those days, the products of De Dion, Bouton were temperamental, to put it mildly. But at least they were available, and in considerable quantities, to any would-be motorcycle manufacturer. There were customers in plenty, each with his own idea of the best way to design a motorbike. Indeed, one of the features of motorcycle design during this period was the variety of positions on the machine that were allocated to the engine. Some were mounted over or alongside the front wheel, others over or behind the back wheel, still others somewhere in between. The main problem for such manufacturers, most of whom had more enthusiasm than engineering knowhow, was how to fit a continuous drive belt to couple the engine's crankshaft to one or other of the road wheels. An even more serious problem—at least for a two-wheeler travelling at more than about 16 km/h (10 mph)—was that of stability. As the present-day rider well knows, a motorcycle with an engine mounted over one or other of the road wheels becomes unstable at speed; a front-mounted engine, in particular, tends to make the front wheel slide outwards at corners.

The matter of engine location was settled, once and for all, by Michel and Eugene Werner, two Russian exiles living in Paris. During the 1890s they had tried various engine positions, none wholly satisfactory. But in 1901 they introduced a model with the engine located low down in a specially designed diamond-shaped frame (similar to that of a pedal cycle) between the road wheels. At one stroke they had effectively conquered the problem of stability and had significantly lowered the motorbike's centre of gravity.

Many fundamental engineering problems affecting the reliability and performance of motorcycles were tackled, although not always successfully, during the first few years of the 20th century. One of the most difficult was the problem of ignition. In most motorcycle and car engines of this time the petrol vapour in the cylinder was ignited by an apparatus called a battery trembler coil. This produced a shower of sparks in the combustion chamber at the beginning of the power stroke, one of the sparks usually serving to ignite the explosive mixture. Maximum power, however, is delivered to the crankshaft only if the gas is ignited at exactly, not approximately, the right moment–the timing being measured in minute fractions of a second. The ignition problem was solved, in principle at any rate, in 1903 by the German engineer Robert Bosch, whose high-tension magneto system was designed to generate a good, fat spark to ignite the vapour at the precise moment required. The magneto, together with the sparking plug, which had been developed the year before by one of Bosch's colleagues, was quickly adopted by all the major manufacturers, and it remains to this day the basis of car and motorbike ignition systems.

Early Racing

Until well into the 20th century the technology of the motorcycle and motorcar was pioneered in continental Europe. The backwardness of Britain in this field was due at least in part to the imposition, ruthlessly upheld by magistrates, of speed limits on public roads. An act of Parliament, limiting speeds to 6.5 km/h (4 mph), was passed in 1865; a second act, passed in 1896, raised the limit–but only to 19.5 km/h (12 mph). Such speed limits gave motorcyclists small advantage, if any, over the pedal cyclist or the man on horseback, and offered manufacturers little incentive to invest in development engineering. By contrast, the limit-free continental roads enabled enthusiasts to organize regular inter-city races, and the prestige and sales potential of the winning machines spurred the European manufacturers into investing heavily in designers and engineers. Another reason for the lack of a specifically British contribution at this stage was the activities of the British Motor Syndicate, headed by Harry Lawson, which from 1896 onwards purchased patent or distribution rights in a variety of continental powered vehicles and components, with the intention (luckily frustrated) of cornering the entire British market in motorcycles and cars.

The situation was to change swiftly, however, when in 1905 the Auto-Cycle Club organized motorcycle trials on the Isle of Man, where there was no speed limit, to select entrants for the International Cup races that by now were held annually on the Continent. The trials, and later the Manx Tourist Trophy (TT) races, set a trend that has continued to this day: the development and improvement of road bikes on the basis of racing machines that have established themselves in the arena of international competition.

BELOW This 1913 Zenith Gradua's multi-ratio belt-drive system made it an almost invincible competitor in hill-climbing competitions.

RIGHT The staid appearance of this 1913 BAT with wickerwork sidecar belies the marque's formidable TT record before World War I.

Edwardian Days

The fierce competition of the international races soon laid bare the technical weaknesses of the motorcycles of Edwardian days. The twisted rawhide drive belt, prone to stretching and sudden breakage, gave way to V-section rubber-and-canvas or leather belts. As speeds increased, the need for better suspension quite literally made itself felt: the jarring and jolting not only made the machines difficult to control at speed but also caused many frames to fracture. One early answer to the suspension problem was the front-end parallel-slider fork with compression springs, developed by Alfred Drew in 1906, which greatly improved the handling and steering properties of TT and grand-prix machines. This and other improvements in suspension quickly found their way onto road bikes.

Gearing was the next major engineering challenge to be tackled. Ordinary road bikes–and indeed many racers, too–had for long been fitted with pedals because, lacking gears, they needed the help of muscle power to get them over the steeper hills. For racing machines the problem was put into stark focus by the decision of the Manx authorities to hold the 1911 TT on the island's fearsome Mountain Circuit. The British firms of Rudge-Whitworth and Zenith had earlier attempted to solve the problem with unsophisticated, if technically sound, multi-ratio belt-drive systems. It was at this point that American motorcycle technology (until then almost unknown in Europe) intervened decisively for the first time. For some years Oscar Hendstrom and George Hendee, founders of the Indian motorcycle company, had been striving to perfect a two-speed countershaft transmission incorporating a clutch. When satisfied with its performance they integrated it with a drive chain and rear-wheel gear sprockets in place of the belt-drive system. Technically the Indian system was superior to any used by European manufacturers. That it was also superior in practice was dramatically proved in 1911, when Indian V-twin four-strokes took the first three places in the Manx TT.

Most road and racing motorbikes of Edwardian days were powered by four-stroke engines using a variety of cylinder arrangements–V-twins and parallel twins as well as single-cylinder types. The principle of the two-stroke engine was already known at this time, but research into the type had yielded little practical success. Potentially the two-stroke offered an obvious advantage: since its induction, compression, power, and exhaust cycle is completed in one revolution of the crankshaft instead of two (as in the four-stroke engine), at a given engine speed its power stroke occurs twice as often as in the four-stroke. This potential became a demonstrated fact in 1912, when Frank Applebee easily won the Manx Senior TT astride a twin-cylinder two-stroke made by Alfred Scott. (In motorcycling, as elsewhere, fashion has a habit of repeating itself: today, after being out of favour for some years, two-stroke machines, now water-cooled and with rotary valves, have re-established their former dominance of the road-racing circuits of the world.)

About this time a number of engineering companies, realizing the growing importance of the motorcycle market, began to specialize as manufacturers of components such as engines, gearboxes, front forks, and frames. Among the best and most widely used of such products were the lightweight engines of Villiers and JAP and the gears of Sturmey-Archer. The response to this ready availability of components was immediate. Scores of individuals or groups who had access to a lock-up or spare garage space suddenly formed companies and began to assemble the readymade components into marketable motorcycles. Most of them just as suddenly went out of business. For although it was possible to produce adequate 'bitsas' from bought-in proprietary components, the future lay with the companies who had the resources and vision to develop teams of specialist designers and engineers and who were prepared to test and improve their products in the hard school of international competitions. World War I effectively wiped out most of the 'bitsa' companies; indeed, even some of the greatest names in European motorcycles were crippled by the economic consequences of the war.

During the European conflict the centre of motorcycle innovation moved to the United States. In 1911 one of the greatest American motorcycle engineers, William Henderson, had swiftly gained an enthusiastic following with a machine powered by a four-cylinder in-line engine. This was a greatly improved version of a similar engine made by Pierce-Arrow, a company already established as a maker of fine cars. During the next few years four-cylinder engines were adopted by Indian, Harley-Davidson, and most other American manufacturers, including the Ace company formed by Henderson after his original firm had been taken over by Excelsior. By the end of the war the Americans were undisputed leaders in motorcycle engineering and had pioneered the use of such significant improvements as the twist-grip throttle control, the drum brake on the rear wheel, the foot-operated clutch, the starter motor, and electric lighting.

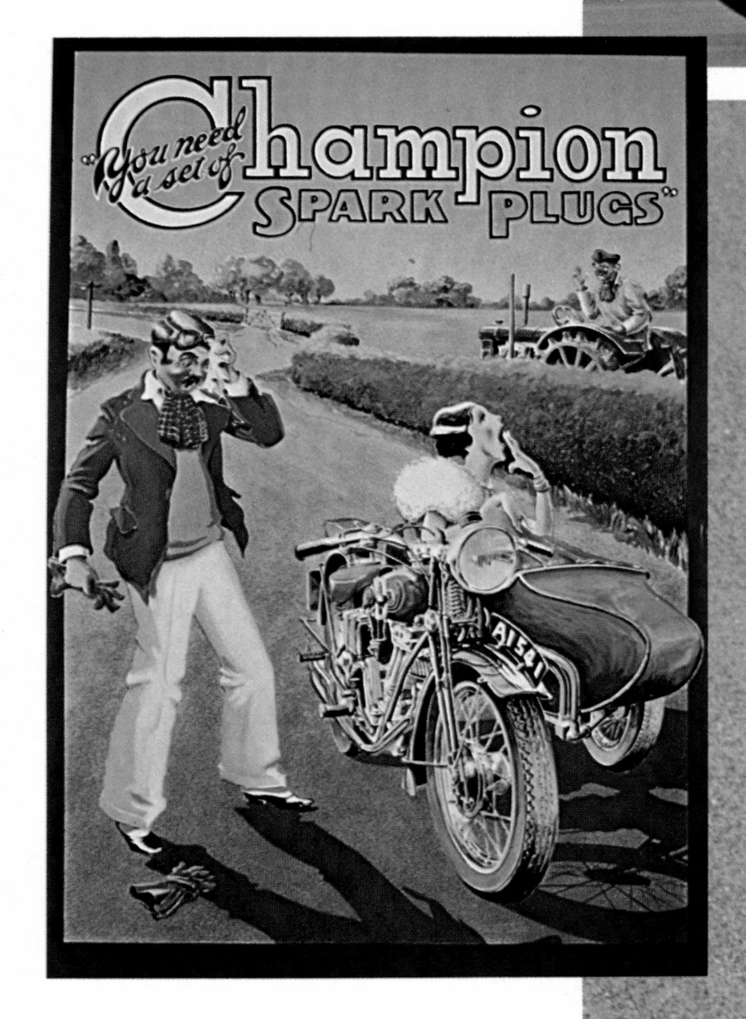

ABOVE A typical early 1930s advertisement.

TOP LEFT An AJS 348 cc, single-cylinder of 1926. That year a similar AJS lapped the TT circuit at over 113 km/h (70 mph).

RIGHT The 1920 Indian with 'flat-head', side-valve, V-twin motor.

TOP RIGHT The formidable 1,301 cc, four-in-line motor of the 1924 Henderson–a late version of a classic American motorcycle.

Indian
EL 5172

Between the Wars

Ironically, it was the European manufacturers who were chiefly to benefit from these improvements. In spite of its technical inventiveness, the American motorcycle industry entered a period of decline after the war–a decline foreshadowed, as we now know, on that day in 1908 when Henry Ford had unveiled his Model T. The American public was to vote decisively in favour of four wheels instead of two, and Ford's Tin Lizzie continued to sell by the million until it was replaced in 1927.

The European motorcycle and car manufacturers also benefited enormously from the tremendous technological leap forward, especially in metallurgy, that had been forced upon the contending nations by the needs of war. In particular, harder steels and a variety of light but strong alloys helped to transform the durability and performance of motorcycle engines. Harder steels made possible much stronger camshafts and valve springs; the new alloys enabled designers to make pistons from aluminium instead of much heavier iron or steel, leading to much higher engine revolutions and greater power output than ever before.

These improvements in engineering materials went hand in hand with significant advances in design technology. By the early 1920s side valves were being replaced by overhead valves operated by pushrods; this configuration in turn gave way, in the mid-1920s, to overhead-camshaft (OHC) engines–a type still to be found under the bonnet of the world's great sports cars.

The German BMW company, which had built some of the finest aero-engines during the war, produced its first motorcycles in 1923. It is an enormous tribute to the firm's quality of manufacture and to the inherent soundness of its original designs that both its engine configuration–horizontally opposed twin-cylinder four-stroke–and its use of a shaft instead of chain drive are still features of all BMW road and racing bikes.

By the mid-1920s Italian manufacturers were also beginning to make an impression on the racing scene. Moto Guzzi, in particular, was building a range of advanced lightweight OHC four-strokes. Their reliability and great speed were demonstrated in 1926, when Pietro Ghersi won the Manx Lightweight (250 cc) TT and set a new lap record of 101 km/h (63 mph)–only to be disqualified for making a false declaration about the type of sparking plug he was using.

The manufacturers were by now building enormous power into their racing engines, and multiple gears allowed riders to use this power at optimum revs whatever the road speed. Until the late 1920s, however, the hand-operated gear lever, mounted alongside the petrol tank, prevented even the best rider from exploiting fully the engine power and gearing flexibility at his disposal. One reason was that movement of even the best-designed hand levers was laborious and slow; another was that, while he was changing gear, the rider was controlling his racer with only one hand–a very dangerous thing to

do if one was dicing with the rest of the pack around a tight, bumpy corner on the Isle of Man circuit.

The answer to the problem was the positive-stop foot-gearchange mechanism invented by Harold Willis, a racing engineer at Velocette. Its decisive superiority to the hand-change method was proved for all time in 1928, when Alec Bennett's and Willis's Velocettes came first and second in the Junior (350 cc) TT. Thereafter all the successful racing marques adopted the foot gearchange, and today, of course, almost every motorbike apart from automatics and a few mopeds uses this system.

By the mid-1930s most of the engine features we find on the latest machines had been designed, tested, and race-proved by one or other of the leading manufacturers. Two-stroke engines with rotary valves had been pioneered by Scott and Vitesse. The three-cylinder, double-OHC four-stroke–a configuration that today is the special pride of Kawasaki and some Italian roadsters–was pioneered by Moto Guzzi as long ago as 1930. A year or two later another feature of the modern superbike, the four-stroke with four valves per cylinder instead of two, was introduced by Rudge.

Suspension is another area in which today's machines were anticipated, in general principles if not in refinement, by the road racers of 40 years ago. The first successful hydraulically damped telescopic front-wheel springs were fitted in the late 1930s to the works racers of BMW and Norton. Only in the field of supercharging, exploited most successfully just before World War II by Gilera, BMW, AJS, and Velocette but banned after the war by the racing authorities, has TT and grand-prix practice not found later expression in two-wheel roadsters.

By the outbreak of World War II, Britain's long record of success in the racing field had secured for it commercial domination of the motorcycling world. Many of the touring machines of that time–the Triumph vertical-twin Tiger 100, the Ariel Red Hunter, the BSA Gold Star, and the prestige machinery of Norton, Matchless, and AJS–were among the finest expressions of contemporary motorcycling technology.

The Lull Before the Storm

When peace came in 1945 the British industry shrugged its shoulders, complained about the quality of low-octane 'pool' petrol, and continued building bikes on the lines established successfully before the war. Typical of the post-war generation of British models was Norton's 1947 500 cc Model 7–a fast but noisy and bone-shaking vertical twin.

But the days of British, and indeed European, supremacy were numbered. In a symbolic sense, the watershed was the Manx race meeting of 1954. Nothing especially sensational marked the occasion. In the Senior TT Norton stemmed what in the next decade was to prove an irresistible tide of success for Italian Gileras and MV Agustas; AJS dominated the Junior TT, while the very fast German NSUs turned the Lightweight classes into a procession. But the real portent of the future was not on the circuit but among the spectators–the presence of a man who had a very special interest in the nature and performance of the racing machines. Although few knew it at the time, his interest was to prove disastrous for the traditional centres of motorcycle supremacy in Britain and elsewhere. His name was Soichiro Honda.

LEFT During the 1930s George Brough created a legend by building 'specials' powered by proprietary engines from JAP, Matchless–and even the Austin 7 car. In its gutsy, V-twin-engined form the Brough Superior roadster was capable of well over 160 km/h (100 mph), and specially prepared versions held the lap record at Brooklands before the circuit closed during World War II. This 998 cc SS100 of 1939 was the last of the line, but beautifully preserved Brough roadsters remain among the most coveted collectors' items.

KMR 384

BIKES FOR EVERYONE

LEFT Two significant examples of the post-war trend towards cheap, simple, lightweight motorcycles. The BSA Bantam (on the right), a 123 cc, single-cylinder two-stroke, was introduced in 1948 and became the most successful British machine in its class. The Honda 50 cc, four-stroke 'step-through', first seen in Britain in 1959 (the model here, on the left, is a later version), formed the vanguard of the Japanese motorcycle invasion of Europe, dominating the moped market.

IT has been estimated that, since the birth of the motorcycle 90-odd years ago, at least 2,000 companies (and possibly many more) have ventured into motorcycle manufacture, and that somewhere in the region of 560 of these were registered in Britain alone. In a highly competitive market, only those companies with imaginative managements, innovative design engineers, and successful competitions shops have endured. Survival has hinged on sporting successes and on continual development of new models that have kept pace with–or preferably anticipated–changes in fashion. Over the years, the overwhelming majority of motorcycle manufacturers have failed on both these counts. Most have gone bankrupt, while a fortunate few have managed to sell their assets to more profitable competitors.

Until about 25 years ago the British motorcycle industry, as we have seen, was the most successful in the world, not only in terms of the technical excellence and sporting prowess of its products but also in terms of the total number of manufacturers producing sound and saleable motorbikes for the international market. Today the British industry is in ruins. There are many reasons for this, and by no means all of them have to do with the quality of the machines produced.

The beginning of the decline can be traced back to World War II, which put paid to a number of established companies with excellent reputations: Rudge, Sunbeam (unless one counts the post-war BSA-built Sunbeam S7 and S8 models), Brough, New Imperial, and many others failed to survive the war. The best placed were those companies which had worked during the war on government contracts (not necessarily building motorbikes) and who consequently had sufficient capital after 1945 to invest in post-war production to meet a steadily increasing demand for relatively cheap, economical, and reliable two-wheeled transport.

By the early 1950s Villiers, Excelsior, and British Anzani were building proprietary lightweight, two-stroke engines from 98 up to 250 cc, and this enabled a number of small motorcycle companies to establish themselves in the ride-to-work, lightweight touring motorcycle market. Excelsior themselves, Norman, Dayton, DMW, Greeves, Sun, Francis-Barnett, and James were among the best-known firms to use these proprietary engine-gearbox units in a range of machines that were almost identical in performance, with only their colour schemes, small variations in design of frames and suspension, and the name plates on the fuel tanks to prove that they were built in different factories.

The Villiers 8E and 9E single-cylinder two-stroke and 2T twin-cylinder engines were to remain for some years the mainstays of the lightweight motorcycle industry in Britain. Even companies as renowned as DOT and Cotton, which had done well in pre-war TT races with their highly successful four-stroke racers, had to rely on Villiers engines to continue production after the war. Only the larger manufacturers such as BSA, Triumph, Norton, Ariel, Royal Enfield, Velocette, AJS, and Matchless could afford to build lightweight motorcycles powered by engines of their own design.

Perhaps the most successful of all these lightweights was the BSA Bantam. The design for this machine was claimed from the German DKW factory as part of Britain's war reparations, and thousands of pale-green, 123 cc, single-cylinder, two-stroke, three-speed models were churned out by the Armoury Road factory.

The first of the BSA Bantams, designated the D1, appeared in 1948–9 and was adopted by the Post Office as the standard transport for telegram boys. The beauty of it was its simplicity. Petroil lubrication, flywheel magneto ignition, and direct lighting meant that so long as the correct mixture of petrol and oil was poured into the tank, a prod on the kick-start gave reasonably reliable transport at minimum cost. The front telescopic forks were undamped and the rear subframe was solid, although a plunger rear-suspension frame was also offered.

In order to keep pace with competitors, BSA had to revamp the Bantam a number of times, first increasing the capacity to 148 cc and, finally, to 175 cc. The last of the line, the Bantam D14, had a four-speed gearbox, contact-breaker/coil ignition, a generator for battery lighting, full swinging-arm suspension at the rear, and front telescopic forks. Such was the versatility of these machines that devotees of the marque even took to racing them under formula regulations laid down by the Bantam Racing Club.

Another success story also came about through the claiming of designs under the guise of war reparations. Ariel motorcycles of Selly Oak, Birmingham, was granted rights to manufacture the German Adler 250 cc two-stroke twin engine. Ariel incorporated this in a monocoque, pressed-steel-construction frame, truly unique for its period, which had a dummy fuel tank in the usual position and the real one situated beneath the saddle (an idea quite recently adopted by the Japanese because, by lowering the machine's centre of gravity, it improves low-speed handling). The entire engine, apart from the frontal area, was enclosed in panelling, and the rider was protected against the weather by leg-shields and a windscreen. The Ariel was well in advance of fashion in other respects: its flashing indicators, electric clock, and other fittings were not to become standard items on motorbikes until the Japanese invasion a decade hence.

With some justification, Ariel called this machine the Leader. It was, however, a little too far in the lead: its reception from an ultra-cautious motorcycling public was decidedly cool, and it was not until it had been stripped of all its panelling and called the Arrow that it was finally accepted as a 'real' motorcycle. For a period of four or five years in the early 1960s the Arrow and its tuned sports version, the Golden Arrow, sold well in Britain. But they found few buyers abroad and, with growing competition from imported machines and the need to develop internationally saleable products, they were finally abandoned by Ariel's parent company, BSA.

The most depressing characteristic of the British motorcycle industry in the 1950s and early 1960s was its complacency. Until this period, things had gone very much its way, in both the British and the international markets: it seemed to assume that whatever it built would be eagerly accepted by a transport-hungry world. Above all, it failed to invest adequately in new engineering and design technology: the Bantam and the Arrow – both essentially 'borrowed' from the Germans – were scarcely complimentary to British innovatory prowess. Not surprisingly, the next development – the scooter boom – caught the British industry unprepared.

By the late 1950s the German NSU company had virtually killed off the Excelsior and other British auto-cycles with its astonishingly lively 50 cc single- and two-speed mopeds, which sold in huge

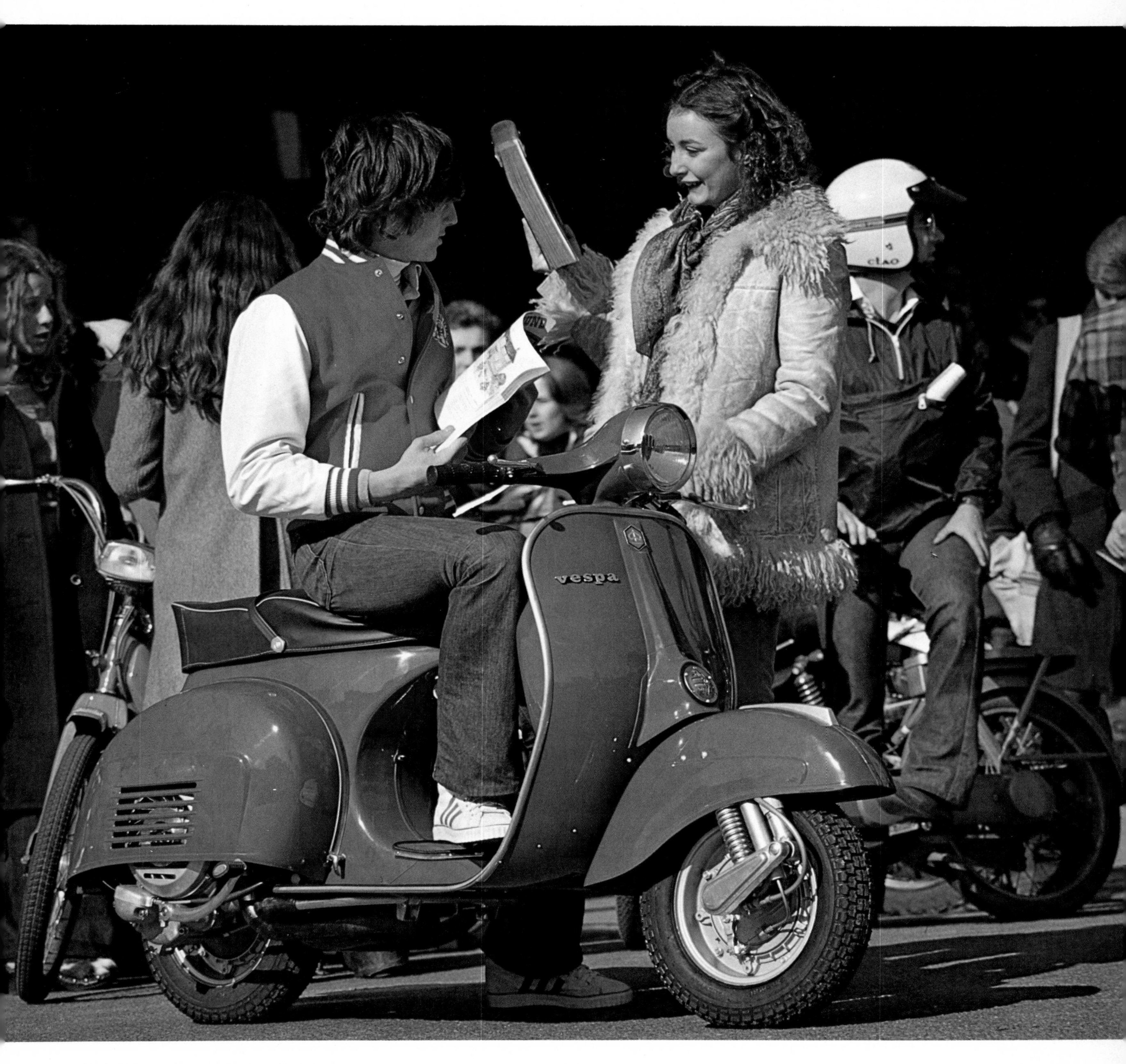

LEFT This Norton Dominator 77 of 1953 was one of a long line of post-war vertical-twin Nortons, from the four-stroke Model 7 of 1947 to the 850 cc Commando of the 1970s. The Dominator, a 500 cc model, featured the 'featherbed' frame with swinging-arm rear suspension and telescopic front forks.

ABOVE The 'scooter' boom of the early 1960s was led by the Italian Vespa and Lambretta machines. With small, fat-tyred wheels (giving a low centre of gravity), a step-through design, and mechanical parts concealed behind panelling, the scooter proved as attractive to women riders as to men. Although scooters have been overtaken in popularity by the moped, this 1970s Vespa shows the almost ageless quality of its 20-year-old design.

quantities to workers fed up with pedalling a bicycle to and from their places of work. Hard on the heels of NSU's invasion an almost toy-like machine, with tiny wheels and a panelled body, arrived from Italy.

The scooter, as this type of machine came to be called, was pioneered by two Italian manufacturers. The first of the type, the Vespa (Wasp), carried its 125 cc two-stroke engine with built-in gearbox beneath the off-side of two bubble-shaped panels enclosing the rear wheel. A unique design feature used the transmission casing as the pivoting-arm suspension on which the rear wheel was mounted. The second Italian scooter, the Lambretta, also had a small-capacity two-stroke power unit with shaft drive to the rear wheel.

Within three years the scooter market boomed. Quiet, clean, highly manoeuvrable in traffic, and both easy and good fun to ride, the scooters rapidly opened up a whole new area of two-wheeler ownership. At long last young ladies could ride a powered machine wearing a skirt and ordinary shoes: the 'step-through' design allowed easy mounting and dismounting, the front panel, or apron, gave full protection against dirt and rain on the lower half of the body and, with a wind-shield added, it was possible to keep clean and tidy.

By the mid-1950s the British manufacturers woke up to the fact that Vespa and Lambretta were carving chunks out of their motorcycle sales, and hurriedly embarked on a crash scooter-building programme. They met with scant success: they were too late and, in any case, few if any of the British models could hold a candle to their Italian rivals. BSA built a Sunbeam scooter based on a modified Bantam 175 cc two-stroke engine. Triumph used the same engine in their Tigress scooter, which was also available with a 250 cc, twin-cylinder, four-stroke power unit. Velocette's contribution was powered by a two-stroke engine with twin, horizontally opposed cylinders; it was a clumsy giant compared with the nippy Italians. Even the Dayton and DMW scooters, using the highly efficient Villiers engine-gearbox units, failed to make much impression on the market. By now both the Vespa and Lambretta had not only reached a very high level of development: equally important, they had become highly fashionable in a predominantly middle-class market, acquiring a social cachet their British rivals could not aspire to.

Ironically, yet another blow to the British motorcycle industry was itself British: Alec Issigonis's Mini. One of the most significant cars of the post-war era, the Mini was introduced in 1959 and soon demonstrated that its 850 cc engine had only a marginally greater thirst for petrol than some of the large-capacity motorcycles – and, moreover, the car cost only a little more than the big two-wheel roadsters. Many motorcyclists switched allegiance and bought a car.

The Japanese Invasion

Meanwhile, on the other side of the world, the Japanese motorcycle industry was flourishing. The multi-million population of Japan had an insatiable appetite for lightweight, powered two-wheelers of any description, and, consequently, anybody with enterprize and a reasonably well-equipped engineering workshop could make their fortune.

Soichiro Honda was just such a person. In 1946 this 40-year-old Japanese engineer bought a cheap lot of army-surplus stationary two-stroke engines and with

RIGHT An important recent development in the ultra-lightweight market is the 'sports' moped – its attraction for young riders being that in looks (if not in performance) it is obviously kin to the motorcycle proper. One of the most successful examples of the type is the 1977 Yamaha FS1E, a 50 cc, single-cylinder two-stroke with a four-speed gearbox and a top speed of about 73 km/h (45 mph).

12 other workers set up shop to convert the engines so that they would fit onto and drive push bikes. By 1949 Honda had designed his first complete motorcycle, a small-capacity two-stroke which he named the Dream. Constant re-investment of profits ensured that within two years Honda was building and selling more than 250 machines a week. In 1951 he abandoned two-stroke designs to produce his E-model four-stroke Dream, the first in a long line of four-strokes to be produced over the next 25 years.

LEFT An evening meeting of members of the South London branch of the BSA Owners' Club. Motorcycle clubs, especially those devoted to individual marques no longer in production, have become popular in Britain since the war. Typical activities include rallies, in this country and abroad, and expert restoration of old machines.

BELOW Suzuki's A100M is the next size up from the sports-moped class, its 100 cc motor giving improved acceleration and top speed. Japanese sports mopeds have a high standard of finish and include wing mirrors and flashing indicators among items fitted as standard equipment.

In spite of financial problems, Honda realized that he had to gamble everything if he hoped to capture the largest share of the home market. He designed and produced his first step-through utility motorcycle, the Cub, in 1952, and the following year he embarked on a massive re-tooling programme which brought him to the verge of bankruptcy. Fortunately his company survived the crisis and by the end of 1953 was manufacturing up to 1,000 Benly 90cc single-cylinder, four-stroke motorcycles a month.

Honda then set his sights on the world export markets. Hence his visit in 1954 to the Isle of Man, where no one, least of all the British manufacturers, realized what was in his mind as he studied the racing machines of the most successful motorcycle-manufacturing countries. He decided that grand-prix racing was the finest publicity platform for any motorcycle manufacturer who wished to sell his products worldwide.

The small-capacity motorcycle market in Europe, with the exception of Italy, was wide open for exploitation, and, by 1958, Honda motorcycles had designed, built, and tested the 50cc step-through C100 and sold well over 20,000 of the machines in a year. Some filtered through to Britain, where Hondis, the importers, attempted to set up dealerships to handle the unusual-looking product. Later Honda was to establish subsidiaries of the parent company in both Britain and the United States instead of relying on the services of importers.

Honda was also developing his lightweight racing motorcycles with which he hoped to capture world titles and acclaim. The Honda race team arrived for its first Isle of Man TT in 1959 with a batch of machines almost totally unsuited for racing on the tricky circuit. Knobbly tyres had to be changed for proper racing covers, and after a reliable if somewhat unspectacular race week the Japanese mechanics, engineers, and riders returned home with many lessons learned.

The following year Honda again competed in the Isle of Man 125cc TT and, although the Italian MV Agustas remained invincible, five of Honda's six machines finished the tough course, close behind the leaders. At the same time Honda was marketing a range of unorthodox-looking 125 and 250cc motorcycles in Britain. The angular finning of the 125cc OHC C92 Benly and CB92 Sports Benly attracted curious glances from British motorcyclists. Square-sectioned rear suspension units on pressed-steel swinging-arms looked decidedly exotic when compared with European tubular frame designs. The absence of damping on the roadster models made them extremely uncomfortable to ride and their poor-quality Japanese tyres proved a nightmare on wet roads. Only the Sports CB92 125cc twin and the Sports CB72 250cc OHC twin machines came anywhere near matching the European-built motorcycles in road-holding.

But there was one thing that amazed the European motorcycling public. The Japanese motorcycles had flashing indicators, electric starters, toolkits, and equipment such as wing mirrors that had rarely before been fitted on European machines except as optional extras. They proved an irresistible sales attraction.

The British industry failed to perceive the threat materializing before its very eyes and, as other Japanese manufacturers sought world export sales, the British lightweight motorcycle market began to be dominated by Honda, Suzuki, and Yamaha machines. One by one the smaller British factories closed down: James, Francis-

Barnett, Norman, Dayton, Sun, Ariel, Royal Enfield . . . the melancholy list grew longer each year.

Britain still dominated the large-capacity motorcycle market through the 1960s with machines powered by essentially obsolescent overhead-valve, four-stroke, vertical-twin engines. Exceptions to the rule were the much more refined German horizontally opposed, twin-cylinder, shaft-driven BMW motorcycles and the magnificent American Harley-Davidson V-twin machines. Each was excellent in its own, very individual way, but too expensive for any but the most dedicated enthusiast to contemplate buying.

LEFT The Triumph Bonneville, probably the most popular machine the company ever made, was built around a vertical-twin four-stroke motor Triumph introduced in the 1930s and eventually built in capacity classes from 350 to 750 cc. This Bonneville 750 of the early 1970s has a five-speed gearbox and a top speed of about 177 km/h (110 mph).

LEFT BELOW In 1970 Britain's answers to the Honda 750 were the BSA Rocket-3 and the almost identical Triumph Trident, with three-cylinder, triple-carburettor, 750 cc engines. Although less sophisticated (and less commercially successful) than the Honda, the Rocket and Trident were superior to it in both top speed and handling. The Rocket-3, shown here, differed from the Trident in the less upright position of its motor.

RIGHT ABOVE A 1973 version of the Honda 750-Four introduced in 1969. Its 750 cc overhead-camshaft engine had four cylinders, each with its own carburettor, an electric starter, and a five-speed gearbox, and took the Honda to a top speed of 193 km/h (120 mph). Effective stopping power was provided by a single-disc front brake.

RIGHT BELOW The Norton Commando 750, introduced in 1968, brought a new smoothness to the ride of British motorbikes, rubber mountings isolating the frame from the engine and transmission and so reducing the effect of the vibrations of its vertical-twin motor.

Power and Speed

As far as the British manufacturers were concerned, as the market demanded faster, more powerful motorcycles, they simply modified or rejigged existing designs either by overboring them (that is, enlarging cylinder diameters) to increase capacity or by fitting twin carburettors, increasing compression ratios, and modifying camshaft profiles to improve engine breathing. Thus the 'soft', touring Triumph 650 cc Thunderbird became the high-performance, sports 650 cc Bonneville; the touring Norton Dominator was transformed into the Super Sports 650 Dominator, and the BSA A10 650 twin was uprated to become the Road Rocket and later the highly regarded but regrettably short-lived Rocket Gold Star.

Unfortunately, the typical 360° vertical-twin motors of such machines were poorly balanced: as engine revolutions increased, so vibration became ever more pronounced. The result was that light bulbs would break, and number plates, mudguards, and even major components of the frame would split under the stress.

Norton attempted to deal with the

problem in 1968, when it introduced the 750cc Commando in which the complete engine and transmission, including the rear swinging-arm suspension, were attached to the main frame by large rubber mountings. This isolated the rider from the vibration, and to a limited degree the system worked; but the special rubber bushes which absorbed the vibration had to be renewed every 16,000 km (10,000 miles) or roadholding deteriorated drastically. (Ironically, the only manufacturer fully to overcome the vibration problem of the classic British vertical twin was Yamaha with its 650cc model. By 1975, after its frame had been remodelled by Percy Tait–once Triumph's chief test rider–the Yamaha XS650, had emerged as a much smoother and more refined vertical-twin than anything British manufacturers were able to offer.)

Triumph and BSA went one better, late in 1968, with the introduction of the 750cc three-cylinder Triumph Trident and BSA Rocket-3. The machines were almost identical except for 'badge engineering' and had basically the same pushrod-operated overhead-valve motor designed by Doug Hele. They were highly successful, especially in the United States, where a rapidly expanding motorcycle market was demanding smoother and more sophisticated machines.

Then, in 1969, Honda stunned the opposition by introducing a brand-new, four-cylinder, OHC, five-speed motorcycle, the CB750. It was said that the project had taken Honda only six months from drawing board to the first production models, whereas the much less sophisticated and technically inferior Triumph and BSA triples had been under development for five years. The CB750 was smooth, powerful, and fast, and its specification (apart from its open-chain drive) was years in advance of anything on the road at that time. Four cylinders, four carburettors, electric starting, five-speed gearbox, front hydraulic disc brake, flashing indicators, full instrumentation including console with warning lights for oil pressure, generator, main beam, and indicators, had until that time been unheard of on a mass-produced motorcycle.

Honda launched the model with brilliantly aggressive salesmanship. To prove beyond doubt that the new machine was fast and reliable as well as technologically very advanced, Honda entered a specially prepared version of the CB750 in the Daytona Classic 200 race–and won. The modern era of the large-capacity superbike had been well and truly launched.

BELOW The three-cylinder configuration popularized by BSA and Triumph is now used extensively by Japanese and Italian manufacturers. This Kawasaki KH250 is the smallest of a range of three-cylinder, air-cooled, two-stroke Kawasakis of up to 750 cc. A good example of the sporty lightweights from Japan, the KH250 has three carburettors and is capable of over 145 km/h (90 mph).

RIGHT These two Yamahas demonstrate the wide choice of machinery available among lightweights. The RD250 (blue) is a two-stroke twin–possibly the last of the line from Yamaha, who dominated the lightweight grands prix of the late 1960s with 'strokers'. A pointer to the future may be seen in the XS250 (red), a four-stroke, OHC twin with similar performance to the Kawasaki KH250. Note the thick-spoked alloy wheels, now fitted as standard on many machines.

BELOW As anti-air-pollution laws are enacted in more and more industrialized countries, some motorcycle manufacturers are abandoning the lively but smoky two-stroke motor in favour of the relatively clean four-stroke. Typical of this trend among the bigger roadsters is the Suzuki GS750, a four-cylinder, double-overhead-camshaft machine with five gears and a maximum speed of over 200 km/h (124 mph).

MODERN
CLASSICS
GOLD WING
Executive
001
LESTER

HONDA
HONDA

SUPERBIKES are nothing new. From time to time throughout motorcycling history machines have emerged whose advanced specification, exceptional quality of construction, or spectacular performance has placed them ahead of their contemporaries—and beyond the reach of all but the most dedicated enthusiast. Some obvious landmarks in this category are William Henderson's trend-setting in-line four-cylinder giant of 1911, the legendary Brough Superior of Brooklands fame in the 1920s and 1930s, and, in the years immediately after World War II, the somewhat unsophisticated but rocket-fast HRD-Vincent Black Shadow.

Yet sheer performance statistics are not the sole criterion of a classic machine. Between the heyday of the Black Shadow and the introduction of the trend-setting Honda CB750 in 1969 was the brief ascendancy of the big-engined Triumphs, BSAs, and Nortons. Among the best of these machines was the Triumph 650 Bonneville, introduced in 1959. Although its acceleration and top speed were fairly modest compared with the performance of present-day superbikes, its handling qualities and speed of response to the rider—especially after its suspension had been refined by Doug Hele—are still recalled with enthusiasm by its many admirers. Beautifully maintained 'Bonnies' are still to be seen on the roads of Britain and elsewhere—especially in the United States, where the exploits of American riders on earlier Triumphs at Bonneville Salt Flats, Utah, had been acknowledged in this model's name.

Although they never inspired the same affection as the Bonneville, the Triumph Trident and the very similar BSA Rocket-3 were arguably the best machines ever produced by the British motorcycle industry, especially after March 1975, when the NT160 Trident was fitted with disc brakes at front and rear and an electric starter. Both models offered high-speed cruising in reasonable comfort, and in their three-cylinder engine configuration they anticipated a trend that was later to find more successful expression in some Japanese and Italian superbikes, as we shall see in the following pages.

Norton, meanwhile, responded to the threat of Honda's CB750 by overboring the engine on their Commando to 850cc. By the mid-1970s the Norton, too, was fitted with an electric starter, hydraulic disc brake on the front wheel, flashing indicators, and many of the other items offered—and relentlessly promoted—by Honda, but it came up with nothing to match the highly efficient, very complex, but reliable Japanese motor. It was rather like offering cosmetics when major surgery was needed. Already by the late 1960s the quality of the big Japanese machines had won for them the lion's share of the crucially important North American market; now they were poised to conquer Europe as well.

ABOVE An authentic superbike, the 1948 Series-C HRD-Vincent Black Shadow was the fastest production machine of its day, with a top speed of over 200 km/h (125 mph).

Honda had set the pace, but now Kawasaki, Suzuki, and Yamaha were following close behind in the race to produce bigger, faster, and more sophisticated superbikes. The only significant European challenge to the Japanese big four came from the Italians and from the German BMW factory at Stuttgart.

In the superbike field the Italian manufacturers, unlike the British, not only learned the Japanese lesson in time but were prepared to take on Honda and the rest and even to challenge them in engineering excellence. Today, there can be little doubt that the Japanese continue to lead the world in motorcycle research and technological innovation, while the quality of finish on their machines—and even their superbikes are essentially mass-produced—remains astonishing. But, for many people, the finest Italian motorcycles offer not only great power and speed but also the ultimate experience in pure handling and in that essential but indefinable quality of 'feel' that makes the true aficionado totally at one with his machine.

One of the few large-capacity motorcycle manufacturers that remained almost uninfluenced by Japanese thinking until quite recently is the German car and motorcycle firm of BMW. During the middle years of the 1960s BMW almost ceased motorcycle production, mainly as a consequence of the sales slump that occurred in the United States and Europe. But the firm's fortunes recovered during the early 1970s with a fine new range of 500, 600, and 750cc models. While they have not neglected recent trends in superbike engineering and design, the most striking characteristic of BMW motorcycles is the sheer quality of their construction and finish; although not perhaps the most exciting of the big machines, they have a fair claim to the title of 'the motorcyclist's Rolls-Royce'.

This last observation serves to remind us of changes in what might be called the sociology of the motorbike. The modern classics described on the following pages are special in more ways than those of sheer size and performance. After all, there are still plenty of enthusiasts around who are capable of transforming the performance of quite ordinary roadsters by judicious tinkering of one kind or another. The significance of the present generation of superbikes lies in the fact that they are aimed directly at a section of the public that motorcycle manufacturers have never before catered to on this scale. The machines offer not only tremendous road performance but a high degree of mechanical refinement, luxury, and comfort—at a price that places them beyond the reach of the traditional motorcycling public. We have to think of the modern superbike as a direct competitor of the high-performance sports car, and this is a development that may have profound implications for the motoring world in general.

Meanwhile, the struggle for supremacy continues, with bigger, faster, more powerful, and more expensive superbikes being unveiled every year. Let us have a closer look at a few of them.

Honda GL1000 Gold Wing

When Honda announced that it was launching a 1,000cc superbike, most of the press and public assumed that it would be merely a larger version of the fast, glamorous, and world-shakingly successful CB750. Honda surprized them – as it has been doing ever since the company was founded in 1946. That Honda had the formula for success was evident in its early days; and by the time it had reached its 18th year of production the company was making 1.25 million machines a year, exporting almost one third of them, and had become the largest motorcycle manufacturer in the world. At the same time Honda has established a reputation as the greatest innovator in motorcycle technology. On occasions the company's products have been almost too brilliant for their own good – witness the astonishing ultra-lightweight racers of the late 1960s that obliged the Fédération Internationale Motocycliste to change the engine-configuration rules for small-capacity grand-prix machines. At the other end of the scale, Honda has consistently shown the way forward in the superbike field, both in engineering sophistication and in the occasionally gimmicky but always highly marketable array of 'extras' it provides as standard equipment.

The GL1000 is a potent example of Honda at its best. It flouted all the established design traditions of its day with its water-cooled, horizontally opposed, OHC, four-cylinder engine. Almost car-like in construction, with a nylon-toothed belt drive to the overhead camshafts, the motor produces 80 hp at 7,900 rpm. This power is transmitted to the rear wheel via a five-speed gearbox and shaft drive to give a maximum speed of approximately 200 km/h (125 mph). Weighing about 212 kg (570 lb), the Gold Wing is efficiently halted by large twin hydraulic discs on the front wheel and a single disc at the rear.

The many unusual features of this superbike include a dummy fuel tank which houses the electrical equipment, an overflow tank for the water-cooling system, and an auxiliary kickstart lever – which doubtless is rarely used in view of its excellent electric starter. Although the petrol filler cap is set in the conventional position on the dummy fuel tank, the actual fuel container is underneath the saddle to the rear of the engine. This makes for a low centre of gravity, which improves the machine's low-speed stability and steering.

While it is neither the fastest nor the quickest-accelerating of the many 1,000cc machines in this highly competitive end of the market, the Honda Gold Wing must assuredly be counted among the modern classic motorcycles. It is a superbly efficient and comfortable tourer that will cruise effortlessly for hours at speeds of 160 km/h (100 mph) or more. The Gold Wing 'Executive' shown on pages 26–7 is a customized version of this machine featuring special paintwork and protective fairing, as well as a selection of extra equipment.

Kawasaki Z1000

When Kawasaki Heavy Industries launched the 900 Z1 model it completely outshone the established CB750 Honda. Its 903 cc, four-cylinder, double-OHC motor gave the Kawa a standing 400 m (¼ mile) acceleration figure of less than 13 seconds and a top speed of almost 210 km/h (130 mph). Then came the Z1000.

Technically the very highest expression of air-cooled, four-cylinder, large-capacity motorcycle engine design, the Z1000 has chain-driven overhead camshafts operating directly on shim-adjusted valves, the crankshaft runs on five roller main bearings, and all big-ends on the connecting rods have needle-roller bearings. A five-speed gearbox transmits the power by specially sealed and lubricated roller chain to the rear wheel, and, with twin hydraulic front disc brakes and a single disc at the rear, the Z1000 has quickly built a reputation as a true 'muscle' bike among its contemporary Japanese rivals – a very fast and exciting machine.

Yamaha XS1100

Yamaha's early 500, 650, and 750 cc twin-cylinder, four-stroke roadsters were far from inspiring in either outright performance or handling, and had only moderate commercial success. But there were greater things to come: the eight-valve, 500 cc, four-stroke twin was more than a match for anything else in the capacity class on the market, and the XS750 three-cylinder, double-OHC, shaft-driven superbike competed well with the CB750 Honda and BMW R75/7.

At the Paris Motorcycle Show of 1977 the company announced the ultimate in Yamaha motorcycle design for the 1978 season – the XS1100. This 1,100 cc, four-cylinder, double-OHC, five-speed, 95 hp machine has all the trimmings, including shaft drive, cast-alloy road wheels, electric starter, and quartz-halogen headlights, and with a top speed of 225 km/h (140 mph) and a standing 400 m (¼ mile) of less than 12 seconds, it offers virtually race-track performance to the superbike owner.

Suzuki RE-5

It is rumoured that Suzuki spent more than £2 million in developing the Wankel rotary-engined RE-5. Sadly, it has not so far found favour with the buying public even in its improved Mark 2 version.

In principle the Wankel motor is much simpler that the conventional piston because it has only two moving parts – the rotor (equivalent to pistons in a normal engine) and the crankshaft.

When it comes to smoothness of operation, acceleration, and overall performance, the RE-5, with its 497 cc engine, is equal to most motorcycles with engines of 50 per cent larger capacity. This is due in part to the fact that the rotor has three firing strokes per revolution. The RE-5 is built very much to superbike specifications: five-speed gearbox, electric starter, twin hydraulic disc brakes on the front wheels, duplex frame with telescopic front forks, and swinging-arm rear suspension. The motor develops 62 hp and gives a top speed in the region of 175 km/h (110 mph).

YAMAHA
XS
Eleven
YAMAHA

SUZUKI
RE5
ROTARY
SUZUKI

Ducati 900SS Desmo

When the Ducati factory first produced a large-capacity 750 cc, overhead-camshaft, V-twin machine in the mid-1960s, it turned out to be a rather 'soft', flexible touring machine rather than an out-and-out sportster. Although Ducati had a long and glorious history in the competitions field, the company had long since abandoned grand-prix racing as being far too expensive to justify in terms of any possible boost to roadster sales. But then, in the late 1960s, Formula 750 racing was introduced and swiftly took hold in both Europe and the United States. The temptation to compete in this new area of the sport could not be resisted, and the factory returned to the racing scene with a formidably competitive machine.

Ducati's brilliant engineer, Fabio Taglioni, worked on the 750 tourer's 90-degree V-twin motor, greatly increasing its power. The result was the Ducati 750-Desmo, which in 1972 took first place in the highly prestigious 320 km (200 miles) road race at Imola, south-east of Bologna. Imola replicas (roadster versions for sale to the public) were produced in the form of the Ducati 750SS Desmo, and a little later the company uprated its capacity and produced a classic superbike, the 900SS Desmo. (The name 'Desmo', incidentally, is a reference to the *desmodromic* operation of the inlet and exhaust valves – one of a number of engineering innovations that have established Taglioni's reputation in the world of motorcycling technology. On the Desmo, the valves are opened and closed mechanically, unlike the conventional poppet valves, which are operated by the action of springs.)

The Desmo's 864 cc, V-twin motor breathes through two giant 40 mm carburettors. It develops approximately 80 hp and delivers a maximum speed of about 210 km/h (130 mph). Equipped as standard with a racing-style half-fairing, the silver and blue monster perfectly projects its racing image.

Moto Guzzi 850 Le Mans

The illustrious firm of Moto Guzzi established a formidable reputation for racing machinery within a few years of its formation in 1921. During the late 1920s it concentrated mainly on lightweight racers, developing a whole series of advanced, overhead-camshaft four-strokes. In the large-capacity field its name was brought dramatically to the attention of British enthusiasts in 1934, when it persuaded the great maestro Stanley Woods to ride one of its machines in the Senior TT – and Woods obliged by breaking the Norton stranglehold and winning in record-breaking time. The firm was always in the forefront of technological innovation. Carlo Guzzi, its brilliantly adventurous designer, was responsible for producing probably the most sensational motorcycle racing engine in history – the 500 cc, V-eight-cylinder, water-cooled unit with four overhead camshafts installed in a Senior TT racer for the 1957 meeting.

In more recent years Moto Guzzi's name has been closely associated, in the big-bike field, with very fast roadsters designed for effortless, long-distance touring and with machines developed specifically for the great races in the International Coupe d'Endurance series. The *Bol d'Or* 24-hour race at Le Mans is among the toughest events in the road-racing calendar. The motorcycles which compete in it must have not only the great speed, acceleration, and handling characteristics of a short-circuit grand-prix racer but also the strength and inherent reliability to maintain peak performance for a full 24 hours without respite, apart from the briefest pauses for re-fuelling, tyre changes, and minor mechanical adjustments.

The Moto Guzzi 850 Le Mans, the company's latest contender in the superbike stakes, is an aptly named result of a wealth of experience gained in endurance racing. The transverse V-twin motor develops 81 hp at 7,600 rpm, which is transmitted via a five-speed gearbox and shaft drive to the rear wheel. The claimed maximum speed is approximately 220 km/h (136 mph). Unlike most of its competitors in this luxury field, the Le Mans uses the slightly old-fashioned configuration of pushrod-operated overhead valves rather than an overhead camshaft. Two 36 mm carburettors meter the fuel into the combustion chambers. The cast-alloy wheels, now typical of most superbikes, are fitted with twin hydraulic disc brakes at the front and a single disc at the rear. The mechanism of the brakes is unusual in that the foot pedal simultaneously actuates one of the front discs and the rear disc, while the normal front-brake lever on the handlebar operates the other front disc. The system has been used before on other Moto Guzzi big bikes, notably the earlier 850 T3, and has acquired the reputation among many experienced riders of being probably the safest and most efficient in the world.

Laverda 1200

Outside Italy the name 'Laverda' is much less widely known–except to the true aficionados–than those of most other Italian marques or those of the Japanese big four. In the years immediately after World War II Laverda's production was devoted almost entirely to lightweight machines of 175 cc capacity and less. Even in those days, however, Laverda pursued its inflexible policy of racing virtually every type of machine it put into production, and these modest-looking little lightweights chalked up an impressive list of production-machine victories and records. It was in those days, too, that the factory's products gained an enviable reputation for roadholding and handling, for the rugged strength and quality of their frame designs, and for the absence of fashionable gimmicks–all virtues that are evident in the highest degree in their present-day superbikes. It is characteristic of Laverda's general philosophy that even on its most luxurious roadsters it has declined to use shaft drive. Although it is the more sophisticated system, it contributes nothing to performance or handling characteristics–a fact reflected in the continued use of chain drive in the majority of grand-prix racers.

Oddly enough, there was a time some years ago when Laverda seemed intent on following Japanese trends rather than initiating its own. But the company ended that phase decisively when it unveiled an authentic modern classic–the Jota 1000, a very fast and utterly Italian expression of motorcycle manufacture. Its 980 cc, three-cylinder motor developed about 80 hp at 7,250 rpm to provide a maximum speed of about 220 km/h (136 mph). Its thoroughbred lines, advanced specification, and truly magnificent handling established the Jota's reputation as one of the greatest superbikes produced in the last decade.

For 1978 Laverda answered the difficult challenge of improving on the Jota with the announcement of its 1200 roadster. Its specification includes a five-speed gearbox, twin hydraulic disc brakes on the front wheel and a single disc at the rear, electric starting, cast-alloy road wheels, and all the usual trimmings associated with the modern superbike. Although Laverda's central concern, in this machine as in all its predecessors, is with achieving the highest possible quality in agility and handling, the 1200 is also one of the most powerful motorcycles at present on the roads. Its three-cylinder, double-overhead-camshaft motor develops no less than 97 hp, offering a claimed maximum speed of more than 225 km/h (140 mph).

An even more exciting portent of the shape future Laverda roadsters may take can be found in the 1,000 cc, V-six-cylinder racer the company has developed for endurance events such as the *Bol d'Or*, the motorcycling world's equivalent of the classic 24-hours sports-car race at Le Mans, in north-western France.

Benelli 750-Sei

Some years ago Benelli produced, in its 500-Quattro, almost a carbon copy of the Honda CB500-Four. It had the same internal dimensions in the cylinders, and it embodied exactly the same design principles; indeed, if one had erased the name 'Benelli' from the engine castings and installed the engine in a Honda frame, only the most knowledgeable enthusiast would have doubted that it was anything but a Honda power unit.

There were no doubt excellent marketing reasons underlying the 500-Quattro's oriental appearance. However, Benelli was soon to dispel any idea that it was enslaved by other people's ideas when it rolled out the 750-Sei. While its engine's cubic capacity is less than that of most other superbikes, it has no fewer than six cylinders. Developing about 75 hp at 9,000 rpm, the single-overhead-camshaft motor propels the Benelli to a maximum speed of approximately 200 km/h (125 mph).

The motor's overhead camshaft is chain driven from the centre of the crankshaft; the bore and stroke of each cylinder (50mm by 50.9mm) are exactly the same as those on the earlier 500-Quattro. The six cylinders breathe through three 24mm dell'Orto carburettors, and the power is transmitted to the rear wheel via a five-speed gearbox and final chain drive. Twin 280mm hydraulic disc brakes provide the stopping power on the front wheel and there is a single leading-shoe drum brake at the rear.

Riding this six-cylinder motorcycle is an exhilarating experience. The turbine-like smoothness of the motor is scarcely credible to anyone brought up on four cylinders or less, and the rider must keep a close watch on the tachometer (rev counter) to avoid allowing the engine to over-rev. The latest version of the Benelli Sei has basically the same engine overbored to 900cc and a maximum speed of about 220 km/h (136 mph).

MV Agusta 850 Monza

During the late 1950s and through most of the 1960s Isle of Man TT races and grand-prix world championships were won with an almost monotonous regularity by superbly designed and immensely fast double-overhead-camshaft, four-cylinder MV Agusta racers. The 850 Monza, named after the classic road-racing circuit a few miles north of Milan, is obviously and fittingly a descendant of those famous racers – tremendously quick and with the handling qualities of a true thoroughbred. Its heavily finned 850 cc, double-OHC motor has four cylinders (each with its own carburettor) and develops 86 hp at 8,500 rpm. Transmission of power to the rear wheel is via a five-speed gearbox and shaft drive. The claimed maximum speed is in the region of 225 km/h (140 mph).

Virtually handbuilt, the Monza is not only a superbly made machine but a highly exclusive one – a fact amply demonstrated by its price, which in Britain is in the neighbourhood of £4,000.

Harley-Davidson 1200 Electraglide

Massive bikes with big, 'soft' engines are one of the most enduring traditions of the North American motorcycle–a tradition established before World War I by such famous names as Harley-Davidson, Indian, Henderson, Ace, and Excelsior. Of these, only Harley-Davidson has survived; indeed, it is now the only major motorcycle manufacturer in the United States.

The company was founded at Milwaukee by William S. Harley and Arthur Davidson in 1903, and in 1909 it began to build the large V-twin, four-stroke-engined machines on which its subsequent fortunes and world-wide reputation were based. In terms of post-World War II trends, Harleys have remained unique, and that is one reason why the Japanese motorcycle invasion of the United States in the 1960s, although damaging to the company, could not destroy the special corner of the market the Harley had created for itself. About this time, too, the factory joined forces with Aermacchi, an Italian manufacturer of aircraft and motorcycles. The merger led to development of a range of light- and medium-weight machines, both touring models and specially built racers.

Meanwhile, the traditional Harleys continue on their successful way. The 1200 Electraglide is the latest version of a model that is more than 20 years old and of a design philosophy almost as old as the company itself. It is powered by a 1,207 cc, V-twin, four-stroke motor with pushrod-operated overhead valves and a single 38 mm carburettor; power is transmitted via a four-speed gearbox and final-drive chain. Compared with present-day superbikes this is a rather unexciting specification. Moreover, the Electraglide's acceleration and top speed of approximately 180 km/h (112 mph) are modest compared with the big Italian and Japanese bikes–which is hardly surprizing in view of the Harley's all-up weight of more than 320 kg (707 lb).

Essentially, however, such facts and figures are irrelevant to the popularity and affection attaching to this machine and its legendary predecessors. The essence of the Harley lies not in its speed or even its size–although that is impressive enough–but in the quality of its construction and the rugged strength of its motor, transmission, and frame. It is, quite simply, many people's idea of the perfect machine for cruising all day, in virtually armchair comfort, on the long, straight roads of North America.

BMW RS100R

While its machines are no longer contenders in the major road-racing grands prix except in sidecar combination form, BMW (the initials stand for Bayerische Motoren Werke) can claim a long and distinguished history in the field of speed. As early as 1932 a specially prepared machine powered by a 750 cc, horizontally opposed twin motor established a world motorcycle speed record of more than 244 km/h (152 mph); four years later a BMW with a supercharged 750 engine raised the record to almost 280 km/h (174 mph). The years immediately before World War II also saw the company establish its reputation for building superb racing machines, BMWs made their first appearance on the Isle of Man TT circuit in 1937, and two years later the racers crowned their efforts by taking first and second places in the Senior TT, the first supercharged machines to win the 500 cc class.

When BMW introduced its first motorcycle in 1923, it was a 496 cc, horizontally opposed, four-stroke, twin-cylinder machine with shaft drive to the rear wheel, and it was fitted with a primitive version of the modern disc brake. Fifty-five years later BMW is still building horizontal twins with shaft drive, proving that the initial design concept was not only sound but years ahead of its time. The power unit has of course undergone continuous development, one of the major changes in more recent years being an overhead-valve system instead of the older side-valve arrangement.

The RS100R has an engine of 980 cc, a five-speed gearbox, swinging-arm rear suspension and telescopic front forks, hydraulic disc brakes on front and rear wheels, and all the attributes of the big modern roadster, enabling it to keep pace with fierce superbike competition. Introduced in 1976, it is very much a purist's motorcycle. It has evolved by retaining the best of the old ideas and blending them with the latest design concepts. Standard fittings include an aerodynamically designed full fairing and a race-style seat, and little luxuries such as an electric clock, a cigar lighter, and a first-aid kit. The machine has a maximum speed of approximately 200 km/h (124 mph). Although it falls short of some other superbikes in absolute speed, the RS100R will cruise effortlessly for hours on end at over 160 km/h (100 mph) and is unquestionably one of the finest touring machines in the world.

SPORTING MACHINERY

To survive commercially, the infant motorcycle industry had to prove to the buying public that motorcycles (or tricycles) were robust inventions capable of travelling long distances at reasonable speeds and with acceptable reliability. The result was a series of inter-city races on open roads between Paris and Marseilles, and Paris and Vienna, plus the establishment of the International Cup races. All of these conferred great prestige on a winning make of machine and the country in which it was manufactured. The motorcycles used were roadster or prototype roadster models similar to those which the ordinary public could buy at that time.

In fact, there was to be a great affinity between the development of road machines and those used in competition right through to the 1930s and, in the case of the British motorcycle industry, well into the 1950s. What was learned on the race tracks, and in trials and enduros (long-distance cross-country events), was applied sooner or later in the form of improvements to roadster machines. This in turn meant that, with only slight modifications, many roadster machines could be used for competing in motorcycle sport.

Then specialization in design began to creep into all sections of motorcycle sport: the four-stroke engine was superseded by the two-stroke in practically all forms of motorcycle competition, while the frame designers attempted more extravagant innovations to keep the high-performance two-stroke power firmly on the ground.

The outcome of the last 25 years of development in sports motorcycles has been the evolution of a variety of 'breeds' almost wholly unsuitable for anything other than the specific purpose for which they were designed. What was once a fairly inexpensive amateur all-round sport has become a very expensive, highly specialized professional occupation, and only at the motorcycle-club level does the true spirit

LEFT Belgium ace Roger DeCoster aboard a two-stroke CZ, the Czech-built machine that revolutionized the moto-cross scene when it ousted the long-established, heavyweight four-strokes.

of the amateur rider survive. In closed-to-club events, whether they be grass-track meetings, scrambles, or trials, club members will ride any machine they can lay their hands on so long as it has two wheels and a motor that works. If the bike happens to bear a plausible resemblance to a machine specially built for the type of event, so much the better.

So, what is the difference between a trials motorcycle, a moto-cross or enduro machine, a grass-track or speedway bike? Some use almost identical power units, but there the similarity ends . . . .

RIGHT Sammy Miller, probably the greatest trials rider of all, demonstrates on a Honda the kind of control that enabled him to win almost 900 events over 20 years. Miller not only helped trials to achieve international status but was responsible for many of the frame and engine features that are now commonplace on most trials bikes.

BELOW Honda was late to enter the sport of moto-cross but is rapidly making up ground with its two-stroke 'fire engines'—this one a 1977 401 cc model. Note the tremendous clearance between the wheels and the mudguards, an indication of the amount of wheel travel and suspension movement required to absorb the violent impact of leaps and bumps encountered on the rough circuits.

ABOVE Typical–although exceptionally successful–examples of trials machinery in the 1960s, these magnesium-engined Royal Enfields of 350 (left) and 500 cc brought one-time British champion Johnny Brittain many notable victories. The development of high powered but flexible two-stroke engines in lightweight frames, pioneered by Sammy Miller and others, quickly made such heavy four-stroke models obsolete.

Trail Motorcycles

Trial or trail? Many newcomers to motorcycling are confused by these two terms, principally because the machines used for each purpose appear to be very similar.

The difference between the two sports is straightforward: trials riding is a competitive activity, whereas trail riding is a hobby which allows the motorcyclist to get off the tarmac and venture out into the country on the numerous 'green' roads. In Britain the members of the Trail Riders' Association spend weekends away from the congested highways enjoying the pleasures of the open countryside.

The machines they ride have a reasonably high ground clearance, and knobbly trials tyres are fitted to the large wheels to give extra grip. Wide handlebars also give the trail bike a likeness to a trials iron. But there the similarity between the two ends.

The power unit of the trail bike usually has totally different characteristics, with maximum power being produced higher up the rev scale. The trail motorcycle also has a closer-ratio gearbox and less steering lock. The electrical equipment is usually very comprehensive, with flashing indicators, main and dipped beam headlights, stoplight, and full instrumentation including tachometer. This means that the weight of the trail motorcycle would also make it quite unsuitable for trials competitions.

Trail motorcycles are now being built by the majority of the world's large manufacturers and vary in capacity from 50 cc two-stroke mopeds to 500 cc four-strokes. They have been increasing in popularity throughout the world owing to their on- and off-road capabilities which make them equally suitable for road or rough riding.

Trials Motorcycles

Trials riding, or 'mudplugging' as it is sometimes called, is possibly the safest of all motorcycle sports. For years, the motorcycles used in the sport bore a close resemblance to the roadsters from which they were developed. Large-capacity, low-revving, four-stroke roadsters were fitted with larger wheels and knobbly tyres for extra clearance and grip in mud, and heavy steel mudguards were replaced with light alloy. The bikes were given a small fuel tank and seat, wide handle-bars for better control, and a wide-ratio gearbox.

It was a design philosophy which worked admirably in its day. The British motorcycle industry reigned supreme and the large Norton, Royal Enfield, AJS, Velocette, BSA, and Ariel four-stroke singles dominated the sport. Then, in 1962, Sammy Miller, the top trials rider of the 1960s and possibly the greatest ever, designed the Bultaco Sherpa, the first purpose-built two-stroke trials motorcycle, which changed trials riding from an amateur pastime into a professional sport. Miller set the trend and the rest of the motorcycle trials world followed. The four-stroke engine was dead and the lightweight two-stroke was champion of a rapidly expanding motorcycle sport.

Basically, a trials motorcycle can be defined as a machine which has a ground clearance below the bottom of the crankcase/frame of at least 25 cm (10 in); an engine varying in capacity from 125 to 400 cc and developing maximum torque (pulling power) at the lower end of the engine rev scale; and a wide-ratio gearbox of four, five, or six speeds, which allows the rider to make maximum use of engine flexibility on steep inclines or in on-road use between trials sections. Fully silenced and equipped with speedometer and optional electric lighting for road use, the trials motorcycle is registered and taxed.

Although the cost of trials machinery has risen considerably since the introduction of 'works replicas' (versions of competition machines specially built for sale to the general public), trials riding is still a cheap form of motorcycle sport.

RIGHT Dutch moto-crosser Ken Van der Vos aviates on his Husqvarna, a very competitive two-stroke machine from Sweden. Husqvarna, together with Greeves and CZ, launched the modern moto-cross revolution in the 1960s when they introduced the highly tuned two-strokes.

BELOW Typical of the early race-winning two-strokes is this 250 cc Greeves, seen at a Glastonbury moto-cross meeting in 1965. The rider is veteran ace Dave Bickers, an ex-world champion.

ABOVE Two more highly competitive moto-cross two-strokes, this time in the 500 cc class: a 400 cc Maico, from Germany, with rising star Graham Noyce aboard, followed by Andy Roberton on a Spanish 360 cc Montesa.

Moto-Cross Motorcycles

While trials and trail riding are both reasonably sedate off-road motorcycle activities, moto-cross–or scrambling, as it used to be called in Britain–is one of the toughest sports yet conceived by man. It was pioneered in the 1920s by British motorcycle enthusiasts, who would ride their machines to off-road circuits, strip off all unnecessary weight in the form of lights, mudguards, and other superfluous fittings, and then race up to 50 km (about 30 miles) across rough tracks and heathland to the finishing flag.

The development of the telescopic front fork helped to establish scrambling as a serious form of motorcycle sport, and the advent of hydraulically damped swinging-arm rear suspension allowed manufacturers to build motorcycles which could be ridden at high speed with reasonable stability over rough ground.

In the early days British manufacturers relied on the large-capacity, single-cylinder four-strokes, just as they had done when building their trials machines. Brute strength and courage were needed by the riders of the 1950s to handle the massive 500 cc, four-stroke AJS, Matchless, Norton, and BSA scramblers which dominated the scene. There was a 250 cc class, but it was very much the 'junior' class with its low-powered two- and four-stroke machines. Then, in the 1960s, Greeves of Britain, Husqvarna of Sweden, and CZ of Czechoslovakia produced a new generation of 250 cc two-strokes which were highly tuned and were built into lightweight frames with specially developed suspension systems to cope with moto-cross conditions. Racing suddenly became more spectacular and the 250 cc class was rejuvenated. Overbored versions of these lightweights were soon competing on equal terms with the giant four-strokes, and when 350 and 400 cc two-strokes appeared, the big, heavy four-stroke was abandoned.

Moto-cross machines are totally unsuited for road use and so are not equipped with electrics other than ignition systems. They do not have to be registered or taxed and consequently may be used or raced only on private land.

Although they are of the same capacity classes as most trail and trials machines, the highly tuned moto-cross motorcycle engines produce considerably more power. The machine is lighter and has a more flexible suspension system, with far greater travel of front and rear forks, to absorb the fierce bumps and leaps encountered on the moto-cross race circuit.

The greatest strides in the development of moto-cross machines in the past five years have been in frame and suspension design. Cantilever frames with inert-gas shock absorbers permit greater travel of the rear wheel, ensuring that in spite of extremely rough terrain the tyre remains firmly in contact with the ground to transmit full power and maintain speed.

Enduro Motorcycles

In events such as the International Six Days Trial (ISDT), where speed and reliability are necessary to avoid strict time penalties at checkpoints, competitors ride a special breed of motorcycle which has the performance of a moto-cross machine and also the equipment needed to comply with road traffic regulations. This is the enduro motorcycle.

A fully equipped enduro motorcycle carries a spare chain, spare brake and clutch levers, spare inner tubes, a compressed-air bottle for rapid inflation of punctured tyres, and of course a comprehensive toolkit. The competitor also normally carries a number of other useful spares in the pockets of his riding suit, and must be capable of carrying out all manner of mechanical repairs en route.

Enduro machines are built in all capacity classes from 50 cc upwards and compete in the ISDT in different categories according to engine size. These motorcycles are of little practical use to the average road rider and, although they resemble trail bikes, most large-capacity machines are little more than thinly disguised moto-cross racing irons.

Similar machines are used in the United States for desert racing, and it is because of the growing interest in this type of off-road racing that the Japanese manufacturers have turned to building enduro motorcycles to compete in events such as the ISDT. However, it is the East German MZ two-strokes and Czechoslovakian JAWA/CZ enduro bikes that have dominated the sport in Europe for the past 10 years or so.

ABOVE This Czech 344 cc Jawa two-stroke is something of a wolf in sheep's clothing. Its lighting and other equipment make it 'street-legal' (permitted to travel on public roads), but its engine and suspension are of virtually moto-cross specification. This combination of characteristics identifies it as an enduro machine – the Jawa model that won the 1973 International Six Days' Trial championship.

BELOW Similar in general design to a speedway motorcycle and using the Weslake four-valve 500 cc motor that has been a dominant force in world speedway racing, Don Godden's grass-track bike features swinging-arm rear suspension (speedway frames are solid) and a two-speed gearbox (speedway machines have only one gear). Godden, an outstanding grass-track specialist, also races very successfully on a similar machine at Continental long-track meetings, where speeds of up to 145 km/h (90 mph) are reached on the 800 m (½ mile) tracks by machines which have no brakes.

Grass-Track and Speedway Motorcycles

Anybody seeing a grass-track racing machine for the first time could be forgiven if they called it a speedway bike. The styling is very similar, with high, wide handlebars and spindly frame design, and the power units fitted are the same methanol-burning JAWA, JAP, Cole, or Weslake 500 cc single-cylinder four-strokes as are used in speedway.

A grass-track racer has, however, a number of items which are necessary to cope with the difference between a flat speedway cinder track and the bumpier and often faster grass circuit. For a start, grass-track frames have swinging-arm rear suspension, and both front and rear wheels are fitted with small brakes. Also, instead of having a single-speed transmission, as on speedway machines, grass-track racers are equipped with two-speed gearboxes.

Similar to speedway events, grass-track races usually comprise a four-lap dash around a closely marked circuit; but, instead of there being only four riders on the start line at a time, there may be anything up to a dozen or more. Since the riding technique is similar to speedway, it is not surprizing that many speedway riders, including Don Godden and Peter Collins, are also grass-track champions.

The most popular and successful grass-track motorcycles are built by champions Don Godden and Alf Hagon, and formerly by Elstar Engineering, while complete speedway machines (including the engines) are manufactured by Weslake Engineering and the JAWA factory.

Whereas speedway is run along professional lines on permanent shale tracks, grass-track racing remains essentially an amateur sport run on stubble fields or meadowland, usually provided by a farmer who is also a motorcycle enthusiast.

Dragster Motorcycles

To attempt to describe a dragster or sprint motorcycle is an impossible task. Designs and specifications vary endlessly according to the finances, mechanical ability, and aspirations of the designer and builder of the machine. What these motorcycles do have in common is a long, low chassis with no rear suspension and a huge, flat-sectional rear tyre to gain maximum adhesion on the drag strip. As for the rest of the machine, some have gearboxes, others do not; some use a single-speed with slipper clutch, others use more conventional transmissions. Some riders believe that the brute power of a multi-engined machine more than compensates for all the extra weight, while others adhere to the contrary theory that light weight and just one powerful motor are all that is needed for maximum acceleration.

The object of the exercize in building these high-powered monsters of the motorcycle world is to get from point A in a straight line to point B a quarter of a mile (400 m) away in the fastest possible time, and to blow the competitor alongside you 'into the weeds'. There are classes for production motorcycles in sprinting and drag racing, but for most spectators the real excitement comes from watching the supercharged, multi-engined specials.

ABOVE A standing-start quarter-mile (400 m) in 8 seconds or less is the aim of the riders who race the nitro-methane-burning, supercharged dragsters seen at Santa Pod raceway. This 1,132 cc, four-cylinder Kawasaki is one of Europe's most successful dragsters and belongs to Dutchman Henk Vink. Terminal speeds of over 285 km/h (177 mph) are achieved at the end of the drag strip.

Road-Racing Motorcycles

Something of the history of the development of road-racing machines appears in the next chapter, but we should say a word here about the different types of event in the road-racing calendar.

Road racing, the fastest and most glamorous of the motorcycle sports, has more classes based on engine capacity than any of the others. Capacity classes date back to the years before World War I; the first Senior and Junior TTs, for instance, were held on the Isle of Man in 1911. Over the years, as the performances of racers have increased, the classes have proliferated. Today there are world grand-prix championships for machines of 50, 125, 250, 350, and 500 cc. These form the very heart of the road-racing scene – the world of grand-prix stars such as Barry Sheene, Steve Baker, Mick Grant, Kenny Roberts, Walter Villa, Pietro Bianchi, and the rest. In addition, there are the Formula 750 championship; the Internationale Coupe d'Endurance series of long-distance events such as the *Bol d'Or*; the Formula 1, 2, and 3 Manx TT championships, with different capacity limits for two-stroke and four-stroke machines; and a variety of events for production machines (more or less modified roadsters).

The quest for speed is never ending, and present-day racing motors develop prodigious power. The Formula 750 racers, for instance produce up to 130 hp – as much as most 3-litre car engines, and almost double that of an ordinary 750 cc roadster.

BELOW The start of the United States' 750 cc Grand Prix. One of the differences between these machines and ordinary roadsters is that they develop about twice as much power as a roadster engine of equal size. International events for racers of larger capacity than the classic 500 cc grand-prix machines have been one of the most significant trends in road racing in recent years.

TT & GRAND PRIX

ALTHOUGH many consider the Isle of Man to be the birthplace of road racing, motorcycle and motor-tricycle races began on the Continent, where De Dion, Bouton and Werner machines competed in races staged between Paris and such distant points as Bordeaux, Marseilles, and even Vienna.

The speed limit on all British roads made it impossible for the newborn motorcycle industry to race or test its products to the full. Some British manufacturers took their motorcycles to the established cycle-racing tracks at Crystal Palace and Canning Town in London, or to Aston Villa in Birmingham, but the short, paved tracks did not provide the answer to their problems.

In 1904 the Royal Automobile Club approached the Isle of Man authorities for permission to stage trials on the island, where there were no speed restrictions, for the European motorcar races sponsored by the American newspaper magnate James Gordon Bennett. The Manx Government agreed. At once the Auto-Cycle Club, the forerunner of the Auto-Cycle Union, requested similar facilities for the motorcycle industry so that it might run eliminating trials to select a team for the 1905 Coupe Internationale, an annual endurance race organized by the Fédération Internationale des Clubs. The Governor of the Island, Lord Raglan, gave his consent and, in spite of sparse support, the A-CC ran its International Cup eliminating trials in 1905 on the Isle of Man with reasonable success. The winner was J. S. Campbell on a 6 hp Ariel-JAP, second was Harry Collier on a 6 hp Matchless-JAP, and third was Charlie Franklin, also on a JAP-powered machine.

LEFT At 60.5 km ($37\frac{3}{4}$ miles) the Isle of Man Mountain Circuit is by far the longest and most challenging road-racing circuit in the world. Here a lone rider urges his machine through a series of fast bends on the climb towards the Guthrie Memorial and the Mountain Mile. Behind him, and already far below, lies Ramsey Bay.

ABOVE In 1911, the first year the dreaded Mountain Circuit was used, the Indian company competed in the Manx TT and made a sensation by taking the first three places. The Indians' decisive superiority lay in the hill-climbing performance provided by their two-speed transmission with final-drive chain. Here Charlie Franklin, who finished second, poses with his machine before the race.

This British team competed in the International Cup races, which were run near Paris, but was hopelessly outclassed by the Austrian and French motorcycles. However, the following year was to prove a turning point in the fortunes of the British motorcycle industry. When the Austrian Puch motorcycle company won the International Cup races at Putzau, Austria, and it was discovered that they had been cheating by giving impermissible assistance to the winning two machines, there was an uproar. The races were abandoned and the FIM was dissolved.

On the long train journey back from Austria to Britain, the Collier brothers, Freddie Straight, secretary of the A-CC, and the international jury representative, the Marquis de Mouzilly St Mars, began discussing the future of road racing. They wanted to stage an event similar to the International Cup races on the roads of Britain, but with the refusal by Parliament to allow the closure of public roads for racing, the situation seemed hopeless. However, the marquis promised that, if a venue could be found, he would provide a trophy for the winner of the race.

Discussions continued but the problem of venue remained unresolved until finally it dawned on the A-CC that, as they had held their International Cup race trials on the Isle of Man, the obvious solution would be to organize a full-scale closed-roads motorcycle race there. To their joy, the Manx Government agreed to the proposal.

The A-CC wasted no time in formulating the regulations needed to specify precisely the types of motorcycle that would be permitted to race in the Isle of Man event. First, they had to be touring motorcycles as sold to the general public. They could be twin- or single-cylinder machines, as it was planned to have two race classes, and there was to be no engine-capacity or machine-weight limit.

However, there was an extremely strict rationing of fuel which required single-cylinder machines to be capable of a minimum of 144 km (90 miles) per gallon, with a minimum of 120 km (75 miles) per gallon for the twins. This demanded the use of engines that were amazingly economical compared with today's fuel-hungry GP power bikes–and even in Edwardian days it effectively ruled out the giant-capacity specials which had begun to dominate the flat-track circuits on the Continent.

The First Manx Circuit

The next stage was to plan a suitable course for the races. It was no good following the RAC car-trials route over the Snaefell mountain track because none of the single-speed, belt-driven motorcycles of that period would have had any chance of completing the climb. Instead, the A-CC plotted a circuit which ran from the ancient Tynwald mound at St John's along the Peel Road towards Douglas to join up with the present-day TT circuit at Ballacraine. The course then struck northwards through Laurel Bank and Glen Helen, uphill past Sarah's Cottage, along the Cronk-y-Voddy straight, through Barregarrow and Rhencullen, and into Kirkmichael. Here it turned sharp left at the entrance to the village to head southwards along the coast road to Peel, where it turned eastwards on to the home straight for St John's.

The plan of campaign for that first TT race was five laps of the St John's circuit, a compulsory 10-minute rest to refuel and fettle machines and refresh the riders, then a further five laps to the finish: a total of 253 km (158 miles) of sheer torture for riders on unsprung machines that were little more than motor-assisted pedal cycles. The circuit consisted of unmetalled, flint-strewn, rutted tracks with hills steep enough to test the stamina of both men and machines.

It was cool, wet, and blustery on 28 May 1907, when the 25 competitors waited to push or pedal their motorcycles away in pairs at one-minute intervals from the start line outside the schoolhouse of St John's. A crowd of locals stood and watched the peculiar gathering, more disinterested than enthusiastic and certainly unaware that they were witnessing the start of a tradition which was to become one of the greatest attractions in the world of sport.

Only 10 men completed the arduous race; but as the exhausted riders were helped from their machines, all were exalted by their achievements. In spite of punctures, broken belt drives, hair-raising slides, and numerous other hazards, such as straying animals and spectators wandering onto the circuit, the meeting was considered a tremendous success by everyone concerned.

Winner of the single-cylinder class was Charlie Collier on his JAP-engined Matchless at an average speed of 61.15 km/h (38.22 mph). He took 4 hours, 8 minutes, 8 seconds to complete the course, 11 minutes ahead of Jack Marshall on a single-cylinder Triumph. Rem Fowler finished third to win the twin-cylinder class on a Peugeot-powered Norton, and related the frightening story of having to ride through a wall of fire caused by another machine which had crashed on the course ahead of him. Freddie Hulbert finished fourth overall on another single-cylinder Triumph.

Surprisingly, the Triumph machines were the only ones without pedal assistance, and this became a point of discussion when plans for the 1908 TT races were drawn up. If Charlie Collier had not had the benefit of pedal assistance on his Matchless, might Jack Marshall have won instead? To avoid any dispute, Freddie Straight and the A-CC stipulated that no pedals were to be allowed in future. Also, some members of the A-CC considered that the fuel-consumption allowance had been a little liberal, so for the 1908 TT races the maximum fuel consumption was raised to one gallon per 160 km (100 miles) for the single-cylinder machines and 128 km (80 miles) for the twins.

Marshalling around the TT course had also been a little slapdash during the 1907 event, with pedestrians and animals proving a hazard to the speeding riders. To give all race marshals the power needed to carry out their duties without question, Lord Raglan swore them in as special constables–establishing a tradition that has continued to the present day.

With pedals abolished for the 1908 TT races, Jack Marshall proved the critics right when he won the event by almost four minutes from Charlie Collier, in spite of having to stop to repair a puncture and change an exhaust valve. He completed the race in 3 hours, 54 minutes, and 50 seconds at an average speed of 64.78 km/h (40.49 mph). The third rider home was a captain in the Royal Navy, Sir R. K. Arbuthnot, who had taken leave especially to ride his Triumph in the TT races.

The fame of the TT races spread and, with further alterations to the regulations for the 1909 races, whereby the capacity of the single-cylinder motors was limited to 500 cc and that of the twins to 750 cc, plus the lifting of all fuel restrictions, entries for the TT doubled in number.

Initially, the twin-cylinder motorcycles had been regarded as being less reliable than their single-cylinder competitors, but technological progress at this time was fairly rapid and the Collier brothers both realized the advantages to be gained from the extra engine capacity and the fact that all machines were now competing on level terms for one major award in the TT race.

Abandoning allegiance to their single-cylinder, side-valve machine, Harry Collier romped home to victory on a new V-twin Matchless at the remarkable average speed of 78.4 km/h (49 mph). He took 3 hours, 13 minutes, and 37 seconds to complete the course, just under four minutes ahead of G. L. Evans on an Indian V-twin. Third was the single-cylinder Triumph of W. F. Newsome.

BELOW Indian continued to compete in European road races until the end of the 1920s. Here one of the finest riders of his day, 'Flying Freddie' Dixon, negotiates a corner aboard a 3½ hp Indian in the 1923 Belgian Grand Prix. The condition of the circuit, with ruts and sharp pebbles littering its unpaved surface, explains why Dixon (like most other riders of the time) has spare inner tubes wrapped around his waist.

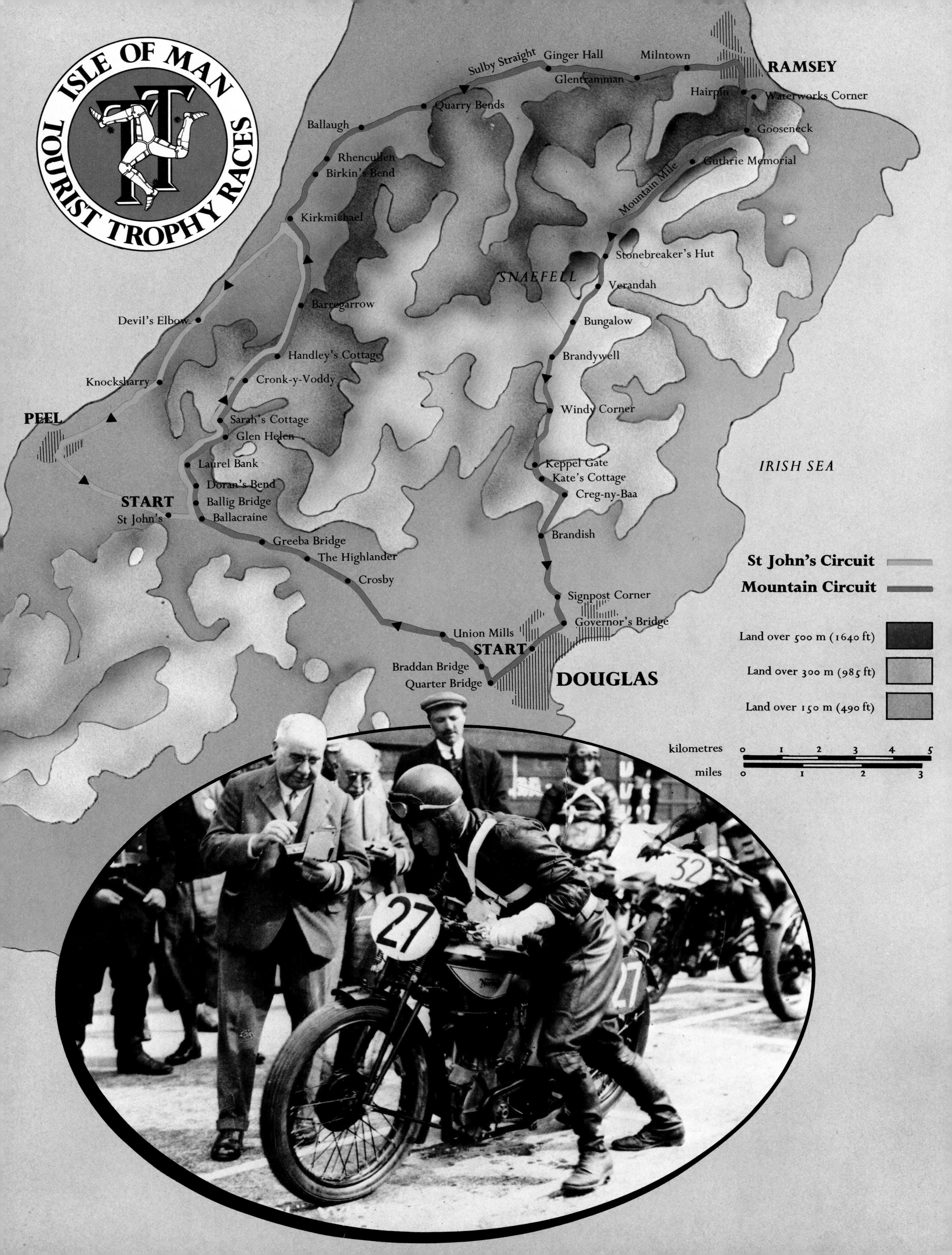
ISLE OF MAN
TT
TOURIST TROPHY RACES
Sulby Straight
Ginger Hall
Milntown
RAMSEY
Glentramman
Hairpin
Waterworks Corner
Quarry Bends
Ballaugh
Gooseneck
Rhencullen
Birkin's Bend
Guthrie Memorial
Mountain Mile
Kirkmichael
Stonebreaker's Hut
SNAEFELL
Verandah
Barregarrow
Devil's Elbow
Bungalow
Handley's Cottage
Brandywell
Cronk-y-Voddy
Knocksharry
Windy Corner
PEEL
Sarah's Cottage
Glen Helen
Laurel Bank
Keppel Gate
Kate's Cottage
IRISH SEA
Doran's Bend
Creg-ny-Baa
START
Ballig Bridge
St John's
Ballacraine
Brandish
Greeba Bridge
The Highlander
St John's Circuit
Crosby
Mountain Circuit
Signpost Corner
Governor's Bridge
Union Mills
START
Land over 500 m (1640 ft)
Braddan Bridge
Land over 300 m (985 ft)
Quarter Bridge
DOUGLAS
Land over 150 m (490 ft)
kilometres 0 1 2 3 4 5
miles 0 1 2 3
27
32

LEFT ABOVE Map of the two historic Isle of Man circuits. Common to both is the section of about seven miles between Ballacraine and Kirkmichael. The old St John's Circuit, relatively flat and about 25.4 km ($15\frac{3}{4}$ miles) long, was used from 1907 to 1910. The Mountain Circuit is more than twice as long and has formidable gradients and corners.

ABOVE A 1926 Scott two-speed, water-cooled, two-stroke twin. Alfred Scott designed the first successful two-stroke racers, and his twin-cylinder, rotary-valve two-strokes won the Senior TT in 1912 and 1913.

LEFT Stanley Woods (Norton) sets off to win the 1932 Senior TT, under the eye of veteran Manx timekeeper 'Ebbie' Ebblewhite. Woods, the most successful pre-war rider on the Isle of Man, also won the Junior TT in 1932 – the first of his three double victories.

A number of interesting things were happening at this time in the development of motorcycling. First, the American Indian motorcycle company had taken the trouble to send a team over the Atlantic to compete in the TT races; second, Alfred Scott entered the first team of two-stroke motorcycles in the history of the event; and, third, back on the British mainland, a motorsport enthusiast, H. F. Locke-King, was busily constructing the Brooklands race circuit on his own private estate at Weybridge in Surrey.

Although still in its infancy, motorcycle road racing was catching on and becoming the accepted means by which to experiment, develop, and test new ideas and machines. If motorcycles could stand the pace of competing in the Isle of Man TT race, then they could certainly be marketed successfully to a growing and enthusiastic public.

By 1910, entries for the TT races had risen to 80 machines. The motorcycle industry had realized the commercial advantages that could be gained from racing success on the Isle of Man. Competition was fierce both on the race track and in the motorcycle showrooms. In four years, the winning times on the 253 km (158 miles) St John's circuit had dropped from 4 hours 21 minutes to 3 hours 7 minutes. Average speeds were now over 80 km/h (50 mph), and when Harry Bowen lapped the St John's course on his BAT twin at 85.04 km/h (53.15 mph), the race organizers realized that a longer, more punishing circuit was needed. The St John's course had had its day.

The Mountain Circuit

In 1911 the A-CC announced a new Isle of Man racecourse, the machine-destroying Mountain Circuit. The 60.75 km ($37\frac{3}{4}$ miles) course, including a long climb up the eastern flanks of Snaefell (426 m/ 1,400 ft), seemed a formidable task to set the motorcycle manufacturers and even the most skilful riders. It was obvious that single-speed, belt-driven machines would not be able to cope with the circuit. For many manufacturers it was back to the drawing board to attempt to design transmissions that would provide variable gearing – low ratios for the steeper hills, high ratios for the faster stretches. Some tried three-speed, rear-wheel-hub gears, similar to those found on present-day pedal cycles; others, such as Royal Enfield, used two-speed all-chain drive, while Douglas sought the answer by using two-speed countershafts on the primary drive from the engine.

It was the American Indian motorcycle company that solved the problem with its countershaft two-speed gears with chain drive to the rear wheel. Indian took first, second, and third places in the 1911 Senior TT race over the Mountain Circuit at an average speed for the winner, O. C.

Godfrey, of 76.21 km/h (47.63 mph).

It should be remembered that at this time the motorcycles competing in the TT races were still very much based on the roadster touring motorcycles available to the general public. There were no one-off specials, only prototype roadsters incorporating design ideas and modifications that were being tested on the race track before being built into the following year's production machines.

The 1920s and 1930s

In those pioneering days before World War I there was no start money for competitors or large prize-money purses for race winners. Competitors such as Harry and Charlie Collier, Howard Davies, and the other early masters were often the men who also designed and built the motorcycles for sale to the public. It was not until the 1920s, when the European motorcycle industry enjoyed a period of rapid post-war expansion, that the true 'works riders' came onto the scene. Norton, Velocette, AJS, Matchless, New Imperial, Rudge, Cotton, Sunbeam, HRD, and

BELOW A beautifully preserved Rudge Ulster 500 cc racer of the 1930s. Although the big Rudges won only one Senior TT (1930), the four-valve-per-cylinder 250 cc Rudges enjoyed many Lightweight success in pre-war TTs.

RIGHT Bill Ivy (Yamaha) flashes through Parliament Square, Ramsey, in 1968, en route to breaking the Lightweight 125 cc lap record at 161.52 km/h (100.32 mph)—the first rider in this class to beat the 'ton'.

9

other successful motorcycle companies could afford to vie for the services of professional or semi-professional road-racing aces such as Freddie Dixon, Stanley Woods, Jimmy Simpson, Walter Handley, and Jimmy Guthrie.

As the European motorcycle industry expanded, so countries such as France, Belgium, Germany, and Italy began to organize their own grands prix. This in turn tempted the British manufacturers to challenge the foreign motorcycle builders on their home grounds.

Yet still the motorcycles they chose to race were development models of roadster sports motorcycles. In fact, it was not until the 1930s that manufacturers began building road-racing specials that were designed to win road races purely for prestige. Such machines were often quite unlike roadsters that bore the same name on their petrol tanks. But this did not lessen the commercial value of successful racers. Ordinary motorcyclists still continued to prefer the products of the TT- and grand-prix-winning factories.

In mechanical and technical terms, almost every possible configuration in the design of the internal-combustion engine had been tried by the mid-1930s. Overhead valves, double overhead camshafts, four valves per cylinder, four cylinders per engine, rotary-valve two-strokes, sleeve-valve four-strokes – at some time some engine designer somewhere had built it to prove that it did or did not work.

At the end of the 1930s, with World War II imminent, national prestige became an important factor in road-racing success. To win races was paramount and, for the first time, the design of road-racing motorcycles departed radically from its original intention of improving sooner or later the stability, handling, or outright speed of the ordinary roadster. The most notable example of this in the late 1930s was the use of superchargers for extra race-winning power. BMW developed a supercharged, OHC, 500 cc twin and Gilera produced their double-OHC, water-cooled, four-cylinder Rondine, while both Velocette and AJS planned double-OHC, supercharged, twin-cylinder, 500 cc machines.

RIGHT Mike Hailwood, riding his poor-handling Honda Four, leaves Governor's Bridge on his way to winning the Senior TT of 1967, in which he established the lap record of 175.12 km/h (108.77 mph). His victory in this race is generally regarded as the greatest performance in the history of the Manx TT. 'Mike the Bike' won nine world championships and 12 TT races before he retired following Honda's withdrawal from racing in 1968. He is returning to motorcycle racing in 1978.

irror
ING
HONDA
4

Road Racing Since 1945

World War II put an end to road racing for almost eight years. At the end of the war the motorcycle manufacturers were able to sit back and take stock of the situation. Pre-war Nortons, Velocettes, and AJS road racers were dusted off, along with a few Rudges and Excelsiors, and in 1947 road racing resumed on low-octane 'pool' petrol.

The Isle of Man TT races recommenced as though the world had stood still for eight years, with the pre-war TT aces Harold Daniell and Freddie Frith taking the honours for Norton and Velocette. However, lessons learned before the war by the Italian motorcycle industry were not forgotten. The FIM banned supercharging for post-war racing, but the memory of the high-revving, super-performance, four-cylinder Gilera Rondine lingered on in the minds of pre-war enthusiasts.

AJS de-supercharged their double-OHC, 500 cc flat parallel-twin racer to produce the sometimes successful 'Porcupine' (so called after the spiky cooling fins on the cylinder heads), while Velocette and Norton continued along pre-war lines with their established single-cylinder 350 and 500 cc OHC racers. Admittedly, both machines resembled the roadsters being produced at the time, but as competition became more fierce on the grand-prix circuits, so the race-development engineers gradually broke away from the roadster production departments. On the other hand, racebred improvements in frames and suspension systems steadily found their way onto the better-quality road machines. Among the most important of these were telescopic front forks, swinging-arm rear suspension, and improved braking.

It is probably true to say that the most decisive separation of racers and roadsters came in the early 1950s with the advent of the Gilera 500 cc four-cylinder racer, followed soon after by the MV Agusta 500-Quattro. National and factory prestige were by now paramount, and victory on the circuits was what mattered.

Unfortunately, this war of attrition on the grand-prix circuits was to have an almost disastrous effect on road racing.

RIGHT Pietro Bianchi (Morbidelli) accelerates out of a corner in the Belgian Grand Prix, on his way to winning the 1977 World 125 cc Championship. The Spa circuit, near Liège, is one of the great European centres of grand-prix racing.

TOP RIGHT Giacomo Agostini, who has won more world championships than any other road-racing star, has now turned to motorcar racing. Here the great Italian takes his Yamaha 500 two-stroke four the shortest way round a corner in the 1977 French Grand Prix at the Nogaro circuit.

MARTINI
FINA
FINA

ABOVE Akimoko Kyohara (54) before the start of the 250 cc German Grand Prix at Hockenheim, near Heidelberg, in 1977. His mount is the interesting two-cylinders-in-tandem, water-cooled, two-stroke Kawasaki. In the background, on a Harley-Davidson two-stroke twin, is Walter Villa (1), 250 and 350 cc world champion of 1976.

RIGHT Barry Sheene, wearing his lucky number 7, corners in characteristic style during the 1977 German Grand Prix aboard the Suzuki 500 cc, four-cylinder, two-stroke racer. Sheene won the World 500 cc Championship in 1976 and 1977. The strongest opposition in his quest for the hat-trick seems likely to come from the resurgent Yamahas.

SUZUKI
TEXACO
HERON
7
CHAMPION
FORWARD TRUST

The cost of developing and producing highly specialized racing motorcycles rose out of all proportion to the benefits or advantages to be gained from extra sales of roadster machines. British manufacturers were the first to feel the pinch and to withdraw factory support from works teams; they were followed in 1957 by the Italian Gilera and Moto Guzzi factories. Grand-prix road racing for a time almost faded into obscurity: the glamour, excitement, and challenge had gone out of the sport as all but MV Agusta withdrew from the scene.

Fortunately, on the other side of the world, there was the rapidly expanding motorcycle industry of Japan, with its sights firmly set on American and European motorcycle markets. When Honda arrived on the Isle of Man in 1961 it had signed many of the top British and Italian road-racing aces. The crowd watched with interest as the Japanese wheeled out a Lightweight 250 cc racer with four cylinders, and then gasped as the little machine proceeded to lap the TT circuit at 159.3 km/h (99.58 mph)–almost as fast as the 350 cc MV Agusta and only 5 km/h (3 mph) slower than the Norton 500 cc machine which won the Senior TT.

Yamaha and Suzuki were the next to enter the grand-prix racing scene and until 1967, when Honda and Suzuki withdrew, the struggle was three-sided, but entirely Japanese, in the lightweight racing classes. The machines bore little or no resemblance to the roadster models that the companies were offering in the showrooms, but with modern designs and resourceful promotion the Japanese industry succeeded both on and off the race track. The only European challenge came from MV Agusta in the 350 and 500 cc classes.

In the late 1960s designs became more and more complex, which practically killed the sport for all but the works riders, until finally the FIM, which dictates what the competing manufacturers can or cannot do, tightened up the regulations. Honda and Suzuki, having dominated the scene, then withdrew in 1967 and road racing was again in danger of losing its popularity. Yamaha, however, continued racing in the smaller 125, 250, and 350 cc classes and took over where Honda had left off, marketing over-the-counter production-racing machines developed directly from its existing roadster models. Yamaha became so dominant that Suzuki was obliged to return to the grand-prix racing scene, with Barry Sheene leading an outstandingly successful team during the 1970s. In early 1978 the road-racing fraternity confidently expected Honda to make a full-scale and very determined return to road racing in order to recoup some of the sales of roadster machines which they have lost to the other marques.

LEFT Today, as in the past, the development of successful racing machines leads to improvements in the quality (and sales) of roadsters. Laverda, intent on challenging Honda and Kawasaki for the European endurance-racing title, unveiled this potent-looking racer at the Milan motorcycle show of 1977. The machine is a water-cooled, 1,000 cc V-6; like other endurance racers, it is equipped with powerful twin headlamps for the night-driving stages.

BELOW A feature of European grand-prix racing in recent years has been the success of American riders such as Steve Baker and Kenny Roberts. Here Baker demonstrates the secret of bodyweight distribution on a fast bend. He seems certain to be a powerful contender for world honours in 1978.

The Future of Road Racing

There seems little doubt, then, that road racing will survive, in spite of continuing crises of one kind or another. As we have seen, the enormous cost of preparing race machines and of supporting them with highly skilled trackside engineers and other staff from time to time discourages even the enormously prosperous Japanese manufacturers from running works teams. But even though grand-prix machinery often bears little resemblance to the ordinary roadster – or even to the superbike – success on the track remains a potent sales factor in the High Street showroom.

Nonetheless, the character of road racing is changing. One sad but significant development is the demise during the 1970s of the Manx TT as a factor in the international grand-prix championship. The Mountain Circuit – with its unique mix of steep hills, narrow and sharply curving country roads, and city-street sections – has always been by far the most challenging of the major international circuits, and many of the top riders have accepted that it is too long and too hazardous to enable the riders to familiarize themselves with its difficulties before racing begins – practice sessions being severely curtailed by the congested grand-

prix calendar. The circuit's heyday ended with the 1972 meeting when Giacomo Agostini, the last of the great masters of Manx, decided to abandon the TT for ever after a fellow Italian rider and close friend had been killed in the Lightweight 125 race. Today the grand-prix world championships have taken over from the old TT and are effectively decided on such famous continental circuits as Spa (Belgium), Nogaro (France), Hockenheim (West Germany), Mugello (Italy), and elsewhere.

Another trend is towards races involving machines of larger engine capacity than that of the classic Senior 500 cc models. Typical are the Formula 750 events that are proliferating in the United States as well as in Europe. A further extension of this trend is the long-distance endurance events for what might be called racing superbikes of up to 1,000 cc and more. Fast developing into a classic in this category is the annual 24-hour *Bol d'Or* run on the historic sports-car circuit at Le Mans. Although the prodigious power and technical sophistication of the *Bol d'Or* raceware are beyond anything the average motorcyclist can see in his local showroom, the remarkable stamina and reliability that must be built into the machines that succeed in this type of race are likely in the long run to have beneficial effects on the quality of motorbikes in general.

NEAR RIGHT Mick Grant demonstrates just how much power there is available from the works Kawasaki 750-triple, two-stroke racer. On this machine he was clocked at a speed of 307.5 km/h (191 mph) on a section of the Isle of Man TT circuit in 1977 and set a new outright lap record of over 180 km/h (112 mph).

FAR RIGHT Phil Read, ex-Yamaha, ex-MV Agusta, and a past world road-racing champion in 125, 250, and 500 cc classes, has been in road racing for almost 20 years and won his first TT, the Junior 350, in 1961. Racing now in Honda colours, Read won the 1977 Formula 1 World Championship TT on the Isle of Man, and is seen here at a midnight pit stop during the 1977 *Bol d'Or* 24-hour race.

635
HONDA
FERODO
FERODO

Being in the right gear, at the right place, at the right moment, with ultra-sensitive use of the throttle to control engine speed, is probably the secret of successful motorcycling. Add a cat-like sixth sense of balance, and it is possible to understand the finesse required to become a champion trials rider.

Observed-trials riding is the slowest and therefore the safest of all motorcycle sports. Speed is not the deciding factor in these events: total machine control and concentration are the skills required to climb slippery slopes, to traverse rocks, boulders, and tree roots, and to negotiate rushing streams. And the riders must tackle all these problems of terrain without stopping or allowing their feet to touch the ground.

A typical one-day observed trial is run over a course approximately 48 km (30 miles) long, divided into 12 or more sections. Each section will usually have three or more 'observed' sub-sections where marshals keep a close watch on each competitor as he passes through a marked-out course. Should the rider have to put a steadying foot to the ground, he is penalized one mark. If he has to 'foot' or assist the motorcycle through the section by using feet and legs while still in the saddle, he is penalized three marks. The maximum penalty is five marks, and this is scored if the motorcycle ceases forward motion, or goes off course and fails to complete the section.

LEFT Trials riding, although the slowest and safest motorcycle sport, demands great skill and perfect balance in the rider, who is penalized if he allows his feet to touch the ground. Here Ian Middleton parts company with his Bultaco in the 1977 Scottish SDT.

At the end of the trial, all the marshals' cards are collected and the scores of each competitor totted up. The rider who has lost the least number of marks is the winner of the trial. If there is a draw, then the rider who has completed most sections 'clean' (without penalty) is the winner.

The big-money international trials scene of today is a comparatively recent development. Until the 1960s, it was very much an amateur sport with no prize or bonus money, just a pewter mug or some other trophy awarded to the winners.

The earliest trials meetings with any tangible connection with the present-day sport began shortly after World War I. Motorcycles had been used by dispatch riders during the war for riding over muddy tracks and rutted, unmade roads, and it was hardly surprising that the skills learned under these conditions should be turned to the advantage of motorcycle sport when hostilities ceased.

In Britain the earliest enthusiasts took to competing against each other on the rough roads that wind their way up well-known hills such as Porlock in Somerset, and Lynton and Beggar's Roost, both in north Devon. Friends were stationed every 20 metres or so to act as observers. Marks were lost for assisting the machine on the climb, with further penalty points being incurred if the motorcycle actually stopped.

Machines ridden in the early days were basically roadster motorcycles equipped with knobbly tyres for extra grip in the muddy off-road conditions. After World War II and for many years, the most prestigious event was the Scottish Six Days Trial, in which competitors would set off each day to tackle different routes and sections in the highlands of Scotland. The motorcycle manufacturers supported the event because of the prestige of being involved and possibly winning. Outstanding riders of the day usually received works support, not only in the provision of factory-prepared machines but also, in many cases, in the offer of a job in the companies' competitions shops. There were no large contract cheques as there are today because most riders were amateur and rode in trials purely because of their love for motorcycling. As the prestige of winning the Scottish Six Days Trial increased, however, so the large British manufacturers began to build better trials machinery, although it was still based very closely on their roadster designs.

RIGHT The Scottish Six Days Trial attracts an international entry, and large crowds concentrate along the most difficult sections of the Highland course. Here Yrno Vesterinen, 1976 World Trials Champion, negotiates a rocky stream on his Bultaco, under the critical eye of another competitor.

BELOW Rocks, mud, even fast-flowing streams have to be negotiated in the cause of 'mudplugging'. Martin Lampkin (Bultaco), member of a renowned Yorkshire motorcycling family, takes to the water in the St David's Trial.

SUNOCO

Purpose-Built Machines

The first dent in the armour of the British four-stroke, single-cylinder trials bikes came in the late 1950s when Greeves (a tiny company in Essex which until then had manufactured invalid carriages) and the DOT motorcycle company (which, by contrast, had had considerable experience of TT racing before the war) produced lightweight two-stroke, purpose-built trials motorcycles. Although they had to use proprietary Villiers motors which were not entirely suited to trials riding, Greeves had a number of successes, with Don Smith aboard one of their two-stroke motorcycles, which should have made the other British manufacturers sit up and take notice.

Then, in 1961, Sammy Miller, who had reigned supreme in trials riding his legendary Ariel 500 cc single-cylinder four-stroke, GOV 132, left the BSA-owned company to design a trials bike for a small Spanish motorcycle company, Bultaco. Using the established Bultaco 250 cc single-cylinder, two-stroke motor, he designed and built the Bultaco Sherpa, a revolutionary machine which was to set the trend for all future trials-bike designs. Almost immediately established design thinking was swept aside and the lighter, easy-to-control two-stroke superseded the heavy and often cumbersome British four-stroke. Demonstration tours of the United States by Sammy Miller and Don Smith increased interest in the sport, and within a few years it had swept Europe and was making inroads into traditional American motorcycle sports.

Surprisingly, it was not until 1966 that the controlling body of international motorcycle sport, the FIM, almost condescendingly agreed to grant championship status to a series of European events. The winner of the first European Trials Championship was Don Smith on his works' Greeves, with Sammy Miller winning for Bultaco in 1968. Smith left Greeves to join another Spanish company, Montesa, to design and build a two-stroke for them, and it was aboard this that he recaptured the title from Miller in 1969. Miller regained it in 1970, and in 1971 and 1972 a first double was achieved by yet another Spanish motorcycle company, OSSA, with Mick Andrews riding the bike he had designed himself.

In 1975 the FIM finally submitted to mounting pressure and announced that the event would be given world championship status. At long last trials riding had earned the credit it deserved and the top riders were in the big-money league. Continental (notably Scandinavian) and Japanese riders have joined the fray but it is still the Spanish two-strokes which dominate the sport.

Six Days of Speed

If you think mudplugging or trials riding is too tame and moto-cross lacks finesse, then what about time trials or *enduros*, as they are called in the United States?

Competitors in time trials set off at one-minute intervals and pace themselves against the clock to average a set speed over a section of road and rough track to reach a checkpoint on time. Every minute late means points lost and the winner is the competitor who arrives at the finish with the least penalty points. The riders are expected to cover sections of anything up to 320 km (200 miles) a day on the road and across some of the toughest and most rugged countryside that can be found.

No outside assistance may be given and running repairs have to be made at the roadside from equipment carried on the bike or on the rider. This means that not only does the rider have to have the stamina of a moto-cross competitor but he must also be a first-class mechanic.

One of the oldest of time trials and an event which still carries tremendous international prestige is the International Six Days Trial. It was first held in Britain in 1913, with the idea of proving to the world that motorcycles were a reliable means of transport and also to encourage manufacturers to build into their machines the necessary stamina and durability to last six days of endurance riding. The routes chosen were not nearly as arduous as those used today, but one has to remember that the motorcycles used then were still basically the roadster models of the day.

Member countries of the FIM entered teams of riders for the ISDT to compete for the International Trophy, and the most important stipulation was that the teams must ride motorcycles manufactured in their own country. This created problems for some countries with only a small motorcycle industry and, in 1924, the Silver Vase Trophy was established as a second award for national teams of three riders entered on foreign-made machines.

Each year a different country hosts the ISDT and to win either the Trophy or Silver Vase is a serious matter of national prestige. In the 1930s there were some tremendous struggles between the British and German teams. Then, after World War II, the British manufacturers had to contend with a strong challenge from Czechoslovakia; and, as ISDT motorcycles became more and more specialized, domination of the sport moved to the West Germans, East Germans, and Czechs. Most riders from the Iron Curtain countries are members of service or factory teams; they ride their motorcycles every day and know every nut and bolt on them. This, and the fact that their countries organize far more enduro events, has made the

Czech and East German teams almost invincible. The only major enduro-type event now held in Britain is the Welsh Two Days Trial and it is from the results of this that the British team is usually selected.

The ISDT is now similar to a six-day moto-cross event. That the men and the machines can stand the pace is incredible. Competitors are allowed only 10 minutes per day to maintain the machines, plus whatever time can be stolen by riders gaining a few minutes on the very tight time schedules. Makeshift repairs to bikes to keep them going are often ingenious: broken frames lashed together with chains strapped round tyre levers, exhaust systems tied on with wire, broken throttles set wide open with speed being controlled by the ignition switch or 'kill' button; anything goes to get the bike to the final checkpoint of the day. At night the machines are locked away in an enclosure called a *parque fermé* and closely guarded to ensure that no one tampers with them, and then the following morning they are wheeled out by the competitors, and they must start within a specified time or points are lost by the riders concerned.

As it is a team event, any one competitor can be responsible for his team's downfall. Consequently, there have been cases of unbelievable courage and bravery by individuals riding with broken fingers, smashed toes, or torn muscles, purely to keep their team in the running for an award. In many cases only pain-killing injections have enabled them to continue.

Enduro riding is probably the toughest motorcycle sport ever devised by man. And it is a sport where only the fittest men and machines survive.

LEFT Not all sections of the SDTs are located in the wilderness, as Rob Edwards demonstrates while easing his Montesa over a mound of concrete in the Scottish event. Edwards, a works rider for the Spanish factory, is one of the elite group who ride successfully as full-time professional trialsters.

LEFT Mick Andrews helped develop the Spanish OSSA trials motorcycle–becoming European Trials Champion in the process. He later transferred his allegiance to the Japanese Yamaha factory and gave them their first victory in the Scottish Six Days Trial. Here he rides a works 400 cc Yamaha in the 1977 World Trial.

BELOW Ulf Karlson, of Sweden, demonstrates the delicate art of 'rock-climbing' while maintaining perfect control over his machine. One of the top dozen contenders for world trials championship honours, Karlson is a works rider for Bultaco.

RIGHT Suzuki was late to enter the international trials scene, but Graham Beamish, a British importer of Suzuki trials machines, is now fielding a strong team of young riders. Here Alan Wright competes in the 1977 World Trial aboard his 325 cc two-stroke Suzuki.

MOTO-CROSS

MOTO-CROSS or *scrambling*, as it used to be called, is one of the most spectacular sports to watch and calls for tremendous physical fitness and stamina from the riders and outstanding strength and reliability from the motorcycles. The sport as it is today is a far cry from its origins, when almost standard roadsters were raced over scrubland circuits.

The first recorded scramble took place in the early 1920s, when a Harley-Davidson ridden by A. B. Sparks won a two-leg race over a 48 km (30 miles) course at Camberley in Surrey. The usual procedure in those early days was for enthusiasts to ride to the race venue and then to lighten the weight of their machines by stripping them of components such as lights, mudguards, and anything else superfluous to the needs of the race. The motorcycles had little in the way of suspension to protect the rider from the ruts and bumps on the course. After one lap of the testing off-road circuit, competitors would relax for lunch, carry out any repairs needed, and then tackle the circuit a second time to decide the overall winner. The results of the scramble were decided on the positions achieved in both legs of the event, with time being the deciding factor in the case of a tie. Much the same system of scoring is used in present-day moto-cross.

Although scrambling continued to develop in Britain, with circuits becoming shorter and manufacturers taking an increasing interest in the sport and slightly

LEFT A good head for heights is only one of many assets essential to success in moto-cross. The major moto-cross courses contain sections where any sensible person would decline to go on foot, let alone tackle at high speed on a furiously bucking and plunging machine. In a sport which seems designed to destroy both man and bike, only the bravest and most skilful riders and only the strongest machines stand the smallest chance of winning.

modifying their roadster designs, it was in France and Belgium in the 1950s that the boom took place. (It was there that the term *moto-cros* was coined. The name soon caught on in Britain and replaced our own, more picturesque term.)

The Continentals saw a future in this exciting off-road sport and established permanent rough-riding circuits about 2 km long with excellent spectator facilities. By the mid-1950s important meetings were attracting anything up to 50,000 spectators. As the crowds paying to see the sport continued to grow, so more prize money could be paid to winning riders, which in turn made the sport more fiercely competitive.

The works-sponsored riders of the 1950s rode giant 500 cc, four-stroke, single-cylinder motorcycles weighing up to 136 kg (300 lb). In spite of being fitted with telescopic front forks and swinging-arm rear suspension, they offered very limited movement of suspension to damp out the ruts and bumps of the circuits. Until the early 1960s the Matchless, AJS, BSA, and Norton bikes, plus Husqvarna from Sweden and FN from Belgium, reigned supreme in the 500 cc class. Even experienced riders had often to fight for control over these powerful but unwieldy machines.

The breakthrough in moto-cross, as in trials, came with the development of a new generation of two-stroke machines, which set the circuits alight with their remarkable handling and speed. Until this time, small-capacity bikes had been under-powered, over-weight, and considered more suitable for beginners; but this new breed of 250 cc two-strokes from Greeves of Britain, CZ of Czechoslovakia, and Husqvarna was so fast and yet controllable that many competitors began entering the senior racing classes on their lightweight machines – and quite a few of them beat the 500 cc racers.

The FIM then ruled that the lightweight machines must remain in their capacity class; but with the trend toward smaller motors already established, the manufacturers of the two-stroke machines simply brought out designs of over 350 cc, which allowed them to compete in the senior events. The impact on the sport was dramatic. In a matter of two seasons, the entire scene changed: of the older British manufacturers' machines, the Matchless, AJS, and Norton four-strokes became obsolete and only the BSA bikes remained to dispute two-stroke dominance.

BSA were fortunate in having the services of two superb development riders: Britain's one and only world moto-cross champion, Jeff Smith, and Vic Eastwood, who had left the AJS team to join BSA. Eastwood had realized that the BSA unit-construction 500 cc, which was reasonably light with a good power-to-weight ratio, was the only remaining competitive four-stroke among British bikes. In fact, when BSA discontinued their moto-cross team at the end of the 1960s, the unit-construction 500 cc four-stroke design was taken up by Alan Clews, who continued development of the machine under the CCM banner and has since enjoyed a fairly reasonable run of success.

There are still many who believe that, with continued development, there could have been four-stroke moto-cross machines

LEFT The tension mounts as riders wait for the starting barrier to drop. The first rider into the first corner has the advantage, as his rear tyre sprays dirt, mud, or stones into the faces of the pack behind. Note the striking similarities of frame and suspension in these machines: more than half a dozen different makes are visible in the picture.

BELOW Vic Allan aboard a Bultaco two-stroke, a leading Spanish moto-cross machine. The treacherously loose ground surface, and the near-vertical drop visible in the background, are typical of the hazards moto-cross riders take in their stride.

equal in performance to any of the current two-stroke models, and some experts consider that the torque and flexibility of the large-capacity four-stroke are potentially much more suited to scrambling than are the high-revving two-stroke designs. This has yet to be proved. Meanwhile, what cannot be disputed is that the development of the two-stroke moto-crosser not only increased the popularity of the sport but brought similar machines within the price range of thousands of enthusiasts. The manufacturers built not only the works competition machines, but also replicas for sale to the general public. The result was that, by the mid-1960s, moto-cross was growing more rapidly than any other sport in Europe. Practically every manufacturer of two-strokes on the Continent saw moto-cross as an outlet for their machines. Montesa, Bultaco, and OSSA of Spain, Maico of Germany, and Puch and KTM of Austria joined the established Husqvarna and CZ companies in the fierce struggle for supremacy in the Continental moto-cross scene.

LEFT Even on relatively smooth surfaces, moto-cross machines spend almost as much time in the air as on the ground. Here, at a German moto-cross, a rider crests the brow of a hill and plunges from bright sunshine into the dark of a wood.

NEAR RIGHT Front wheel up, Roger DeCoster negotiates a relatively easy section in the 1977 British 500 cc Moto-Cross Grand Prix aboard his 376 cc, single-cylinder, two-stroke Suzuki. The Japanese factory hired DeCoster and his fellow-Belgian Joel Robert to help develop their world-championship-winning machines. The pair provided the most formidably gifted spearhead of any of the works teams.

FAR RIGHT From modest and informal beginnings in Britain, moto-cross has developed into an international sport that attracts crowds of over 50,000 to major Continental events. Its cosmopolitan flavour is symbolized in this picture of the Russian ace Genadin Moisseev, winner of the World 250 cc Moto-Cross Championship for the Austrian KTM factory.

BELOW Like a herd of stampeding cattle, the riders hurtle away at the start of the 1977 Spanish Moto-Cross Grand Prix. With the field as closely bunched as this, the inevitable scrimmage at the first corner becomes a major test of nerve and skill.

SAL
ONTESA
250 c.c.
Banco de Vizcay
XIV GRAN PREMIO DE ESP
de Moto-Cross
CAMPEONATO DEL MUNDO

MAICO
CHAMPION
22
22

The Japanese Intervene

This tremendous enthusiasm spread from Europe to the United States, and, with over-the-counter works replicas available, the American market soon boomed. At this point the Japanese manufacturers, who by now were completely dominating the road-racing scene but who had hitherto ignored the potential of off-road runners, realised that here too was a vast market to be exploited. Once more, their intervention was to prove decisive.

Suzuki was the first to plunge headlong into a moto-cross development programme by buying the services of the best available riders, namely world champions Roger DeCoster and Joel Robert. In an enormously expensive crash-development programme, Suzuki designed and built, with the advice and assistance of Joel Robert, a grand-prix moto-cross motorcycle weighing a mere 72.5 kg (160 lb). In one of the most astonishing examples of rapid success flowing from high capital investment allied to engineering knowhow, Suzuki won the World 250 cc Moto-cross Championship at its first attempt. It also captured the title the following two seasons, and then moved into the 500 cc moto-cross scene with DeCoster as its number one rider in the class; the Belgian ace did equally well in the big-bike grands prix.

The Japanese had proved yet again that enormous but carefully planned expenditure on research and development, the signing of top riders, and the use of one-off, hand-built 'titanium specials' secured results. Then, in order to bring a more competitive element back to the sport, the FIM imposed a minimum weight limit of 95 kg (210 lb), which meant that there was no advantage in building highly expensive, ultra-lightweight, titanium-framed motorcycles. Designers turned next to the problems of handling.

The 1970s saw the beginning of renewed efforts to improve frames so that the rear wheel of the bike remained in contact with the track surface no matter how severe the undulations. The result was a tremendous increase in suspension movement, or travel, which in turn brought about problems in damping out the 'bounce' factor of the suspension springs. Damping fluids reached boiling point under racing conditions and lost their effectiveness. Cooling-oil reservoirs were fitted to deal with the problem, and inert-gas suspension was tried.

Yamaha came up with a triangulated rear fork which pivoted at the rear of the main frame and was suspended on a single, very large damping unit. Suspension movement on their machines was approximately 25 cm (10 in) at both front and rear, which meant that the wheels could follow all the undulations of even the bumpiest surfaces with ease. With contact with the ground maintained at all times, the power and flexibility of the engines could be fully exploited and the machine controlled more easily by the rider. It also meant that the moto-cross rider was considerably more comfortable than ever before. Yamaha's 'monoshock' 250 cc moto-crosser was an immediate success and captured the world championship for the Swede, Hakan Andersson.

During the last five years more research has gone into suspension and frame design than into the development of the engines. The enormous significance of this research can be gathered from the fact that the present-day 125 cc moto-cross machines travel as fast as the 500 cc machines, simply because all the power they develop can be put firmly on the track at all times, whereas only part of the power from a 500 cc machine can be used effectively.

TOP LEFT One of the rising generation of moto-cross riders, Graham Noyce is widely tipped for world-championship honours. His full-blooded racing style–here he takes to the air on his Maico–has already brought him success against several of the established stars.

LEFT When Honda entered the moto-cross scene with single-cylinder two-strokes, it looked to the United States, in the shape of Brad Lackey, for its leading works rider. Lackey competes regularly in Europe, where his fearless style has made him a favourite with spectators. Here he seems to be both flying and cornering in a 1977 500 cc event at Farleigh Castle.

ABOVE While the majority of riders in moto-cross leap about on lightweight, if powerful, two-strokes, a number of riders still prefer the gutsy pulling power of the four-strokes. One such rider is Bengt Aberg of Sweden, seen here demonstrating the pace of the 500 cc, four-stroke machine he has helped Yamaha develop from the XT500 overhead-camshaft, single-cylinder trail motorcycle.

LEFT Vic Eastwood and his CCM 498 cc, both carrying their share of Berkshire mud at a 1977 moto-cross meeting at Newbury. One of the ablest British moto-crossers, Eastwood has also ridden bikes for AJS and BSA, and has vast experience as a development rider.

BELOW Although Norton has disappeared from the major road-racing circuits, its name lives on in sidecar moto-cross. Robert Grogg of Switzerland, seen here with passenger Andraes Husser, has won the World Championship with his Norton-Wasp outfit. The heavy-flywheeled Norton 850 cc has proved ideal for this form of moto-cross.

Sidecar Racing

The only section of the sport where the two-stroke power unit has not taken over is in sidecar-cross. Here the big twin-cylinder four-strokes continue to reign supreme. The machines are all hand-built specials that do not have a mass-market sales potential. Consequently, none of the major manufacturers has given support or contracted riders to compete on works specials. Successful riders rely on sponsorship from motorcycle dealers, who are prepared to cover costs purely for publicity value and for the enjoyment they obtain from being involved in the sport.

The big Norton Commando 750 or 850 cc twin-cylinder, four-stroke engine fitted into a Wasp moto-cross frame has been the most consistently successful machine in the world championship over the past few seasons. It is the latest expression of a design principle that has thrown up a variety of heavyweight raceware, including TriBSAs, TriNors, NorBSAs, and other combinations of powerful four-stroke twins that could be built into a moto-cross chair outfit.

Although sidecar-cross racing has failed to attract anything like the enormous investment that the major manufacturers have channelled into solo moto-cross, it is quite as exciting and skilful a sport in its own way. It is a great pity that the enthusiasm of the combination riders and their passengers, who devote so much time and skill to the sport, receives only a fraction of the rewards enjoyed by the professional solo riders.

SPEEDWAY

Speedway racing bears little or no relationship to the motorcycling enjoyed by so many millions on or off the road. The two-wheelers ridden on the 400 m (¼-mile) shale or ice tracks are single-speed, methanol-burning, 500 cc four-strokes that have no brakes, relatively little suspension except on the front forks, and require a unique riding style.

Four riders on equally matched machines release their clutches and hurtle flat out towards the first corner. Jostling for position, forcing other riders off line, it is the bold and skilful rider who gains the advantage. The speedway rider needs courage and superb throttle control to remain in charge of his careering, unbraked motorcycle. Too little throttle and he has dirt blasted into his face by the more daring competitors, too much throttle and he is fighting to control an unleashed beast that is trying to ride him into the safety fence on the outer edge of the track.

LEFT Breathtaking action at close quarters, with cinders flying as the riders go into controlled slides around the oval track: the atmosphere of speedway racing has changed little since this French watercolour was painted in 1928.

Normally there are 13 four-lap races during the course of a meeting, with the five riders, plus two reserves, in each of two teams interchanging riding order so that two riders from each team compete against different riders from the opposing team in every race. The winner of each race scores three points, second two points, and third one point. The team which amasses most points through the individual scores of its members is the winner of the match.

Like football teams, the speedway clubs are organized into leagues, with first and second divisions. The competitors ride two or three times a week at home or away on specially prepared shale tracks and their fans follow them from one end of the country to the other to give their devoted support.

Speedway racing originated in the United States where, on established tracks which were used for pony trotting, dirt riders found the perfect location for a new motorcycle sport. Using the big Harley-Davidson and Indian 1,000 cc V-twins, they rode at breakneck speed around the dirt ovals to entertain the sensation-seeking American public of the 1920s.

After a number of serious accidents, including some fatalities, the capacity of the motorcycles was limited to 500 cc. This reduction in performance caused riders to experiment with riding techniques and, in order to maintain speed through the turns, it was not long before the more daring competitors were broadsiding their machines through the corners with power still turned full on.

A demonstration visit to Australia by the American riders fired the enthusiasm of the motorcycle riders 'down under', who up to that time had been riding on grass tracks, or on concrete. A cinder track, similar to the American pony-trotting tracks, was laid at Maitland and,

RIGHT Steel-plated boots scrub the shale track surface as New Zealander Ivan Mauger, 1977 World Speedway Champion, leads Valeri Gordeev, John Louis, and Edward Jancarz around the 350 m (380-yard) circuit. The sport is truly international, with top-class riders coming from western and eastern Europe, Australasia, and the United States.

BELOW Peter Collins demonstrates the skill that brought him the world title in 1976. Fragile-looking front forks and wheel, no brakes, and a powerful single-cylinder, four-valve motor with only a single gear characterize the contemporary speedway bike. The three overwhelmingly dominant power units in speedway at the moment are the Weslake and the JAWA.

RIGHT The almost crab-like motion of the machines on the corners of a speedway circuit is well caught here as Ole Olsen, the great Danish ex-world champion, leads the tightly bunched trio of Ian Turner, Alan Molyneux, and Jan Henningsen. Note the position of the riders' left feet–quite different from the older leg-trailing technique shown in the painting on pages 82–3.

by 1926, the sport had really caught on, with the first 400-metre track being set up in Brisbane. Here a rider by the name of Cecil Brown is credited with developing the spectacular leg-trailing, broadside riding style.

Enthusiasts in Britain heard about the exciting new speedway craze, and, in 1927, the Camberley Club in Surrey staged the first dirt-track meeting in this country. Unfortunately, the organizers seem to have been a bit slapdash in their research into the sport, and ran the event on a deep sand surface on a clockwise course–totally opposite to the established ideas. However, a month later at Droylesden, near Manchester, a proper dirt-track event was staged, and the following year, with the visit of the Australian speedway promoter Johnnie Hoskins, the foundations of the sport of speedway were truly laid in Britain.

Machines used for dirt-track riding, as it was then known, were little more than roadster motorcycles stripped of all lighting and other ancillaries and with a pair of turned-down handlebars to make them look the part. Some roadsters, notably the old in-line, horizontally opposed, twin-cylinder Douglas, were more suitable than others. The Douglas, in fact, with its very low centre of gravity and long wheelbase, was particularly suitable for the leg-trailing speedway riding technique then in vogue, and it remained one of the more popular and successful competition machines with the British riders throughout the 1930s.

However, as has happened in other forms of motorcycle sport, specialization began to creep into speedway. Machines were adapted in frame design to suit riding styles, and power units were modified and developed. It was found that the 500 cc, single-cylinder, JAP four-stroke, with its steam-train power characteristics, was absolutely ideal for speedway. No gearbox was required because the big single was able to pull from a standstill to maximum revs on the short start-and-finish straight without need for a second gear. Also a short wheelbase with a solid rear-end frame and minimum-movement sprung front forks were perfect for sliding under power through the turns.

The JAP-engined machines were to reign supreme for over 30 years–until the appearance of the Czech-made ESO 500 cc four-stroke in the 1960s. The ESO (which later became JAWA) engine was simple and robust and, with a somewhat shorter stroke, produced more power with even greater flexibility than the British-made equivalent. By the mid-1960s JAP had been eclipsed and JAWA virtually took over the speedway-motorcycle market for almost a decade.

Then, in 1974, the British Weslake Engineering Company, based at Rye in Sussex, designed and built a 500 cc, four-valve, single-cylinder speedway/grass-track motor which was superior to the JAWA in all ways. Don Godden tested it at a grass-track meeting at Lydden in Kent in October 1974 and it beat all opposition hands down.

The Weslake motor rocketed to success and JAWA knew they had to do some drastic redesign work to remain competitive. Four valves appeared to be the answer and both JAWA and the Swedish ERM company now build four-valve speedway motors. However, at present, it is only Weslake who supply over-the-counter power packs with four-valve design. The JAWA unit has been reserved purely for selected riders.

Apart from national speedway meetings held in Sweden, Denmark, Poland, Russia, West Germany, the United States, Australia, New Zealand, and Britain, there are also international 'test' matches between some of these countries. Then there are the individual national championships and, the most coveted prize of all amongst speedway riders, the Solo World Speedway Championships.

Since World War II, it has been New Zealand and Sweden that have dominated the world championships, with Sweden's Ove Fundin and New Zealand's Ivan Mauger capturing the title no less than five times each, followed by Mauger's fellow countryman, Barry Briggs, who has won the title four times.

Fortunately, Britain is now back in the running with riders of the calibre of 23-year-old Peter Collins of Belle Vue and the 1976 British Champion, Malcolm Simmons.

Grass and Ice Racing

Two offshoots of speedway, both of which use machines of similar design, are grass-track racing and ice racing. It could be said, however, that speedway is a derivative of grass-track racing because motorcyclists rode on the rough grass tracks before they were organized to ride as teams on dirt tracks; moreover, many of the best of the present speedway stars

LEFT Probably Britain's greatest grass-track specialist, Don Godden has also had conspicuous success at long-track (800 m) speedway races on the Continent. Here, aboard his Godden-Weslake Special, he demonstrates perfect balance in a controlled slide at a grass-track meeting.

BELOW Wildly spinning rear wheels throw up a curtain of mud at the start of a grass-track race at Lydden, near Dover. Riding technique is similar to that on a dirt track–many of today's speedway stars began on grass–but the machines have two-speed gearboxes, rear suspension, and minimal brakes.

learned their trade on grass.

As for ice racing, this is a motorcycle sport like no other. The machines resemble speedway motorcycles, but the tyres are fitted with needle-sharp, 38 mm ($1\frac{1}{2}$ in) steel spikes which bite into the surface of the ice circuit. These spikes allow the riders to bank their motorcycles at unbelievable angles when cornering. In fact, the riders wear old pieces of motorcar tyres on their left knees and shins which allow them to ride around the turns resting on the knee.

The motorcycles used are single-gear, JAWA-powered, 500 cc four-strokes, which, like ordinary speedway machines, have no brakes and on which the clutch is used merely for starting and the throttle to control the speed.

Ice racing originated in those countries where the winters are hard and thick ice forms on lakes and rivers–although nowadays, of course, events are held on specially refrigerated outdoor or indoor tracks. The sport is dominated at present by the Russians and Czechs who invented it, but it is likely that this spectacular sport will eventually spread much farther afield, especially in those countries where normal speedway has proved enduringly popular.

ABOVE An eastern European development of speedway takes place at sub-zero temperatures on ice. The racing tyres are fitted with needle-sharp spikes, which dig into the ice and allow the riders to bank their machines at incredible angles. Competitors strap a section of tyre to their left knees to lean on while cornering.

RIGHT The steel spikes are fitted high up on the near-side wall, rather than on the crown, of the tyres because the machines race anti-clockwise on an almost circular course. The ice racers are powered by the single-cylinder four-strokes used in conventional speedway bikes, but conditions are often so cold that the motors have to be warmed with a blowlamp before they will start.

Drag Racing

THE fury of a supercharged, triple-engined dragster at full throttle has to be heard to be believed. The noise of 12 unsilenced exhausts is ear-shattering as the rider guns the throttle, drops the clutch, and smokes away from the start line.

The experience is over in a matter of seconds. A quarter of a mile (400 m) is covered in less than nine seconds, with machines attaining speeds in the region of 270 km/h (170 mph). Then, energy spent, they burble back to the pits to be fuelled and oiled, ready to race again.

Many motorcycle enthusiasts find a day spent watching motorcycles accelerating from point A to point B 400 metres away extremely tedious; others, particularly those with a technical knowledge, are amazed at the incredible ingenuity which goes into building a dragster.

Drag races are really won in the workshop. Each motorcycle is an individually built machine incorporating the ideas of its designer-builder, who hopes through his skill to create a winner. Far more hours are spent in the workshop building, modifying, rebuilding, and modifying yet again to improve performance by perhaps a fraction of a second, than are spent actually riding the bikes. The racing is purely a means of testing and proving theories that have been built into the machine in the workshop.

In open drag-racing events, anything goes in terms of specification. Any number of engines may be used in supercharged or unsupercharged form, coupled to single-speed or multi-speed transmissions, and slotted into equally varied frame designs.

LEFT Brian Chapman's *Mighty Mouse* regularly proves that it is not necessary to build multi-engined monsters to compete successfully in drag racing. His machine is based on a 500 cc Vincent Comet, and even in its highly modified form, complete with supercharger, its remarkably light weight has enabled Chapman to give many of his big-bike rivals a beating.

Early Days

However, the sport was not always like this. Like most other forms of motorcycle competition, drag racing had very humble beginnings, with competitors riding almost standard roadgoing machines against the clock over a measured quarter mile.

This early form of drag racing began in Britain in the early 1920s, when it was known as sprinting. There was no side-by-side racing between two competitors, and the results of these sprinting competitions were decided purely on the times of the riders. Today there still exist two separate controlling bodies for the sport: the NSA (National Sprint Association) and the BHRDA (British Hot Rod and Drag Racing Association). The motorcycles raced by members of these associations are basically the same, but in the Sprint Association results are judged against the clock whereas drag-racing results are decided in a knock-out competition of two riders actually racing against each other on the drag strip.

Drag racing as we know it today was imported from the United States, where it had become apparent that sprinting against the clock had little spectator appeal compared with two riders engaged in a man-to-man contest.

The sport began to grow in popularity during the 1950s, when all manner of roadster engines were slotted into lightened frames. Very few competitors at that time were using special fuel, and extra acceleration was achieved by reducing the weight of the motorcycles as much as possible. Everything that could be drilled for lightness without drastically reducing strength was drilled. Items such as 50 cc motorcycle front forks were fitted to 500, 650, or even 750 cc machines, with miniaturized drum brakes being built into the front wheel to reduce weight still further.

As competition became more fierce, the sprint riders turned to supercharging and the use of the oxygen-rich methanol fuel. This vastly increased engine power but it immediately created another problem – lack of traction at the rear wheel. When the clutch was dropped on a supercharged dragster the rear wheel spun wildly on the track. There was no way in which all the extra power could be transmitted to the drag strip using the conventional round-section racing tyres.

Then the Avon tyre company solved the problem by producing a wide, flat-sectioned tyre with no tread and an outer covering of high-hysteresis rubber, a soft, tacky material that grips the road. The tyre was named 'the slick' and with it there was a drastic reduction in standing-quarter-mile times. The only problem was that on dragsters of the period there was a tendency for the tyre to grip so well that the front of the motorcycle would leap into the air and the entire machine would try to loop backwards over the rear wheel.

Frames had to be redesigned, and they became longer and longer and their centre of gravity lowered as far as possible in order to keep the front wheels on the ground. Speeds improved yet again.

As the frames grew longer, so one or

BELOW A burn-out on the drag strip at Santa Pod: competitors melt the surface rubber on their rear tyres to give them improved grip when starting. The effect is dramatic and often entails fitting a new tyre at every meeting – but every aid to speed is crucial when a hundredth of a second can make the difference between victory and defeat.

two rider-designers decided to slot another engine into the frame and build twin-engined specials. The use of fuel blends of nitro and methanol on the supercharged multi-engined specials created rear-tyre adhesion problems and it was not uncommon to see a motorcycle hurtle off the start line and its rear tyre spinning and smoking the entire length of the drag strip.

More rubber was needed on the track surface to stop this loss of power and traction. Slick-tyre widths were increased,

LEFT Another burn-out, this time without the drama of flames. The headlight, fairing, and conventional front forks identify this Kawasaki as a contender in the 'street-legal' production-machine category. The performance of such machines, however, is considerably greater than that of the ordinary roadsters on which they are based.

BELOW Many drag-racing enthusiasts take pride in beautifully decorated machines. But the attractive appearance of Anton de Vos's Kawasaki (seen here by the Santa Pod engine-starting rollers) should fool no one. With two huge 1,000 cc fours hooked in line, it is one of the fastest machines on the strip.

and as the chance of breaking the grip of the new wider tyres was reduced, so all the power had to be absorbed by transmissions. The consequence was that gearboxes and clutches failed and drive shafts snapped. New ideas had to be tried.

The grass-track champion and speedway rider Alf Hagon overcame the transmission problem by getting rid of the gearbox altogether and using a single-speed machine. By incorporating a giant 1,300 cc JAP V-twin supercharged motor in a flimsy but rigid frame, he used a spinning rear wheel almost as a variable transmission. The idea worked and the very flexible and powerful JAP motor blasted him over the standing quarter mile in under 10 seconds, with a terminal speed of around 256 km/h (160 mph).

The Eight-Second Barrier

At this time Britain was still lagging behind the United States, where a special slipper clutch had been developed. This allowed the rider to rev his power unit to the limit for maximum power on the getaway and, as soon as he released the clutch, it would slip to avoid rear-wheel spin, at the same time increasing its grip as the speed of the motorcycle increased.

Twin-engined dragsters were superseded by triple-engined monsters which, with the slipper clutch, brought the standing-quarter-mile times to below the 9-second mark. American ideas were soon to be copied by the British designers, and with engineer-riders of the calibre of John Hobbs, who built the double-Weslake-engined *Hobbit*, the 8-second barrier was broken.

The fastest recorded time is now a little over 7.5 seconds for the run, and British, American, and Dutch riders are vying for the prestige of being the first to break the 7-second barrier. However, as speeds increase, it becomes more difficult to knock even one hundredth of a second off the record.

Track surfaces and tyre adhesion are all-important and for some while riders have been doing 'burn-outs'. This involves propping the front of the machine against a solid wall and spinning the rear wheel until the surface rubber begins to melt owing to friction. At the same time bleach is poured over the tyre and sometimes even petrol is set alight around the spinning rear wheel. When the tyre is hot and sticky it gives its greatest adhesion and the dragster is ready for its run.

'Burn-outs' and 'Christmas trees' are all part of drag-racing jargon. The term 'Christmas tree' refers to the starting system used in drag racing. It resembles a very large traffic light with a red light, three amber lights, and a green light for Go. This is situated between the two competing riders, who watch intently as the lights change from red through amber to green. If a rider can anticipate the green light perfectly by releasing the clutch at maximum revs, he is off to a flying start.

Drag racing has become an extremely expensive sport and most of the top riders manage to build their multi-engined specials only with the help of sponsorship from motorcycle companies. In an effort to reduce costs, racing has been split into a number of classes, including one for ordinary roadster motorcycles.

Although not as exciting to watch, the roadster-class races at least enable ordinary riders to enjoy the sport. In fact, some even ride to the events on their machines, fit the competition numbers, race the machines, and then ride home again—just as the original competitors must have done in the early years of motorcycle sport. In some ways, the history of motorcycling has turned full circle.

ABOVE LEFT The slender spaceframe seems scarcely able to accommodate the two huge supercharged, four-cylinder Honda motors of American Russ Collins' drag racer. One of the two or three fastest machines in the world in 1977, it is among the most strongly fancied to break the elusive seven-second barrier.

ABOVE Although drag racing began in the United States and is still a very big-time sport there, many of the top American riders now compete regularly at Santa Pod against the British stars. One such American ace is Tom Christenson, seen here aboard his Norton-powered *Hogslayer*, which earned its name by regularly overcoming Harley-Davidson-powered monsters. The machine was one of the first to beat eight seconds.

RIGHT The outstanding British engineer-rider in drag racing, John Hobbs blasts off on *Hobbit*, powered by two special Weslake supercharged twin-cylinder motors. One of the sub-eight-seconds elite, Hobbs regularly achieves terminal speeds not far short of 305 km/h (190 mph).

START
TF 8
CHRISTENSON

WESLAKE
KERSHAW

Page numbers in *italics* refer to captions

Acknowledgments

The publishers thank the following individuals and organizations for their kind permission to reproduce the photographs in this book:

All-Sport Photographic Limited (Don Morley) 4, 12–3 above, 22 above, 23 below, 25 below, 26–7, 33, 35 above left, 40 above, 41, 42 above and below, 45 below, 51, 52, 56–7, 57 above right, 58, 62, 64–5, 66, 67, 68–9, 70–1, 74–5, 77, 78 above, 88 below; Vic Barnes 20 below, 30, 35 above right, 37; Michael Carling 46–7; Champion Sparking Plug Company Limited 12; Colorsport 72–3, 89 above and below; Creed Lane Studio 16–7, 20 above, 21, 22 below, 36; Cunningham Hurst Limited 29; Diffusion Photos de Presse Internationale 76–7; Douglas (Sales & Services) Limited 19; Mary Evans Picture Library 82–3; Foto-Nicholls 43, 44 below, 53, 70, 71, 76–7 above right, 80; Jim Greening 40 below, 75, 78–9, 80–1; Robert Harding Associates 8 below; Dave Hawkins 31 above; George Hind 60–1; Brian Holder 78 below; Kawasaki Information Service 24; S. R. Keig Limited 50; Christian Lacombe *(Moto-Journal)* 2–3, 63; Keith Lee 90–1, 92, 93 above, 94, 94–5 above, 95 below; London Art Technical Drawings Limited 5, 59; Leo Mason 1, 45 above, 93 below; Andrew Morland 32; The National Motor Museum 6–7; The National Motor Museum–Robert Harding Associates 9 above, 11, 12–3 below, 13 above right, 14–5; John Nutting 25 above, 34, 60; Mike Patrick 84–5, 86–7 above and below, 88 above; Pictor International Limited 38–9; L. E. Shelley 8 above, 9 below, 48, 49; Jasper Spencer Smith 10, 18, 23 above, 28, 31 below, 44 above; Tony Stone Associates Limited front and back endpapers; Syndication International 54–5; Zefa Picture Library Limited 76 above left.